Mom, I'm a Girl

JUDY GLENNEY

Mom, I'm a Girl

REDEMPTION
PRESS

Published by Redemption Press, PO Box 427, Enumclaw, WA 98022

Toll Free (844) 2REDEEM (273-3336)

Redemption Press is honored to present this title in partnership with the author. The views expressed or implied in this work are those of the author. Redemption Press provides our imprint seal representing design excellence, creative content, and high quality production.

ISBN 13: 978-1-68314-265-2 (Print)
978-1-68314-266-9 (ePub)
978-1-68314-267-6 (Mobi)

Library of Congress Catalog Card Number: 2017934539

DEDICATION

My deepest gratitude to our gracious God who allowed us to have our beloved son, Scott, for nineteen years. He proved time and again His ways are beyond ours. Tragedies are heartbreaking, but many times the vehicle He uses to bring us closer to His precious son, the Lord Jesus Christ. May He use my son to bring many into His kingdom.

Contents

ACKNOWLEDGMENTS

My utmost appreciation to those of you who urged me to embark upon this project. Without your prompting I would never have considered it. But God used all of you (and you know who you are!) to continue to encourage and inspire me to take it on. Thank you for making me accountable when I didn't want to be. Praises be to God who has led me all the way through, as I have trusted Him with every word.

I also want to thank Christi Krug, a very patient and dedicated coach/editor, who worked so diligently with me through the whole process and Joyce Erickson, who graciously did the final editing. Thank you all so very much.

INTRODUCING SCOTT

*For you created my inmost being; you knit me together
in my mother's womb... Your eyes saw my unformed body.
All the days ordained for me were written in your book
before one of them came to be.*
Psalm 139:13,16

Scott Richard Glenney. That was the name
printed on his birth certificate on the day he was born, September 8, 1989. Sydney Royal Glenney was the name printed on
his death certificate, June 5, 2009. His name change was one of
many alterations he underwent on his way to transitioning to
be a girl. But I would like to introduce you to the son I knew.

Barreling down the highway on that early September 8th
morning, my husband was trying to keep his eyes on the road.
Distracted by my groans of every three minutes, he was missing
the beauty of the drive through the San Juan mountains.

"Whatever made you think you had *gas* pains?" he asked, glancing at me. "At ten days overdue, my dear, those pains are not going to be gas," he said. His eyes darted from me to the road.

"I guess I was in a state of denial—I thought I was going to be pregnant *forever*," I said, moaning and squirming. "Besides, they didn't seem like labor pains."

From the very beginning, things weren't always what they seemed with Scott.

As a first-time mother, I didn't know what to expect, even though we had taken all those childbirth classes. We made it to the hospital safely and on time, as I went through only seven hours of labor. After nine (and a half!) months of "expecting," I was ready for the "expected."

"It's a boy," announced the doctor, cradling my newborn son in his arms. I was elated to hear those words as I so wanted a son.

"Oh! My baby!" I cried out. This child, so small, so dependent, so beautiful was now in our care. My husband, Gary, who witnessed the birth, was beaming as all new fathers do. The doctor handed him to Gary. After holding him gingerly, as he was quite unaccustomed to babies, he passed him on to me. *What would the next years hold for all of us?* I thought. Right now, though, I needed to figure out how to nurture this little one. Having never been around kids (much less babies!), I was fearful. But I figured God had placed this very special child specifically in our care. I was going to trust Him to get us through this day and then keep us going for the days, weeks, and years to come.

By trial and error, we made it through Scott's infancy. Several months passed and one day I had Scott in his high chair trying to get him to eat, while he fussed. Gary stepped into the kitchen from his study. Taking off his glasses, he walked over to the table. He put his hands on his hips.

"I can't wait until he can talk and let us know what he wants," he sighed.

"Well, I wouldn't be so anxious," I responded. "If he's going to be anything like his dad, once he starts talking, he won't quit." I looked up at him, smiling. Ruffling Scott's hair, he just smiled, shook his head, and went back to his study.

At nine months Scott was walking and on the move, taking after his mother's propensity for activity. I started taking him for walks and by the time he was a year old, he was walking almost a mile with me down to the store. I would bring the stroller just in case he got tired but inevitably he wanted to push the stroller down the sidewalk. So he did. His little towhead would come up short of the canvas seat back as he reached up to push the handles. He couldn't see where he was going. Keeping on the sidewalk was a chore and I felt like a human bowling-alley bumper. Everything caught his eye. Sprinkler heads were particularly fascinating, so we would stop at each and investigate, becoming familiar with the location. We would practice our vocabulary, saying "water" at each stop. We both craved the outdoors, and the weather in New Mexico was wonderful for outings.

As for talking, well, he grew into that pretty quickly, too. From the time he could sit and listen to stories, I would read to him. I gathered Bible stories with lots of pictures. We would talk about the pictures as I read. I could tell his reasoning capabilities were growing along with his vocabulary. I would make dramatic gestures, using voice inflections, pointing at the pictures. One day I was reading the story of Moses in the desert when he was told to strike the rock for water.

"So Moses took his staff and hit the rock, just like God told him to do!" I exclaimed. "Then, do you know what happened?" I raised my arms with drama.

Scott hesitated for a moment, looking at the picture of Moses with the rod in his hand standing by the rock. Then he cocked his head up at me with excitement.

"The stick broke?"

As I looked down at him, he had a look of pure innocence: big eyes, raised eyebrows, mouth open. Holding back my urge to burst out laughing, I hugged him and said, "Well, it might have this time, but all the people got water as it gushed out of the rock."

Gary was in his first pastorate in Farmington, New Mexico, at a very small church. Since there were no other children Scott's age, I would teach him Bible stories in a class by himself during the adult meeting time. He was about four when we were reviewing the topic of sin.

"Scotty, do you know what sin is?" I questioned.

"Uh, huh, when I do something wrong," he said as he looked down at his chair. He was getting fidgety, kicking his feet back and forth and rocking, so I wanted to get to the point. I bent down to his level and made sure I had his attention.

"What did Jesus do?" I asked as our eyes met.

"He died." Finally, he looked up from rocking in his chair.

"Do you know you can be with Jesus forever if you ask Him to be your Savior and take away your bad things?"

"Uh, huh," he said, looking back down to his twiddling fingers.

I thought it the right time. "Would you like to do that?" I asked, making sure he was looking at me. This is the most important decision anyone can make and I wanted to make sure he understood what he was doing.

"No," he said, shaking his head, no uncertainty whatsoever. I blinked my eyes in a moment of surprise.

Yet, in one way I was encouraged by his answer. He let me know he was making his own decision and not just saying something because it was expected or to please me. Moving on to the next story, I let the matter go. Several months later I brought it up again as we entered into another story about Jesus.

"Scotty, remember when I asked you if you would like to ask Jesus to be your Savior?"

"Yeah," he said. He was coloring at the table, watching me pick up some flannel graph figures. I was putting up various scenes of Jesus—with children, carrying a lamb, and then on the cross.

"Do you remember how we talked about Jesus loving you?" I finished placing the pictures and stood by the board.

"Uh, huh." He put down his pencil and looked up at me. I had added a heart around the picture of Jesus on the cross.

"What did Jesus do?" I asked pointedly.

He got up from his chair and went to the flannel board. Pointing to the picture of Jesus, he said, "He died for my bad things."

Taking his hands and stooping down to his eye level, I asked again, "Scotty, would you like to talk to Jesus and tell Him you believe that He died for your bad things?"

Looking at me and nodding he said, "Yeah."

He folded his hands together and bowed his head. Sitting together we prayed. Very softly, he followed my words, telling His Heavenly Father he knew Jesus died for his sins. In that instant he became a child of God. I knew the angels in heaven were celebrating with me as we welcomed this little one into the family of God. I rejoiced that no matter what happened on this earth I would be eternally bonded to him.

Upon saying "Amen," he got up from his chair and went over to the play table. I knew his abruptness was a simple case of having been still long enough. I was confident that Scott knew and understood the fact that Jesus loved him and died for his sins. As we talked about Jesus being alive and with him always, my heart was singing praises for this precious moment! Little did I know that it would be a great comfort years to come during that fateful day.

Being the "preacher's kid" wasn't easy for Scott, or for me for that matter. I felt under pressure to have a model son. After all, if we were raising our son according to the word we were teaching, it should be reflected in his behavior. Unfortunately, I conveyed that expectation onto Scott. It became part of our "expected" behavior that both Scott and I would wrestle with throughout our lives.

We wanted to teach him about giving to the church at an early age. We didn't pass the offering plate at our church; we set a modest wooden plate by the door where congregants would simply place donations as they entered. It was on a plain stand, about three feet high, just to the side of the door. One morning, Scott had a couple of pennies. Walking over to the stand, I bent down and asked, "Scotty, would you like to put your pennies in the plate to give to Jesus?"

With a simple nod, Scott reached above his head and dropped his pennies into the plate. After the service, before our treasurer took the offering from the plate, Scott went to check. Standing on tiptoes he could just see into the plate. He reached in and took the pennies out.

"Scotty, what are you doing?" I asked, surprised and embarrassed. I gently nudged his hand away from the plate and explained, "Those are for Jesus."

Looking up at me, he said matter-of-factly, "Jesus didn't want 'em."

Trying to keep back a chuckle, I thought, *Well, how do I answer that?*

"I'm sure Jesus will use them," I finally answered. "We'll keep them there to make sure He sees them."

Our family in our church in Farmington.
Scott was about two years old

His favorite pastime was playing with cars and trucks in the backyard dirt pile. He was fascinated with anything with wheels that could roll. Cars were also his preferred object to draw. Drawing was another favorite pastime and many times, Scott would go into Gary's study just to be with his dad. Gary had a pullout board on his desk. With Dad's permission Scott would get out his paper and colored pencils, put them on the board, and go to work drawing as Dad studied. They enjoyed short conversations from time to time, but Scott knew to keep his talking at a minimum because Dad was studying. Mostly, he would be content, interrupting only to make a comment about what he was drawing. His ability to draw different angles and perspectives was astonishing.

Scott drawing in Gary's study

On one occasion, Scott held up a picture of two cars on the road for Gary to see.

One was in the foreground and the other in the background, both in perfect relationship with the distance between them. Trees lined the road, and were diminishing into the horizon.

Scott had always liked the older-model cars. The car in the foreground was the style of a 1954 four-door Chrysler with big fins on the back, red taillights the full length of the fin. Splashes of gold in the form of sunbursts were spread on the trunk and hood over a body color of light green. The wheels were spoked, bright silver. Inside, a pair of black and white dice were visible through a half-rolled-down window. In the background, the second car was visible but down the road a distance. It was a black, chopped two-door roadster, early '30s body style, with the roof modified so the window was about half size. The car sat lower with smaller tires. The oversized front fenders had bright orange flames with a spare tire attached to the trunk.

"Hey, Bug, you're doing pretty good," Gary commented as he leaned over the arm of his chair. He smiled and put his arm around Scott. Then he pointed to one of the cars and asked, "What's this car doing?"

"This car's going to be in a race and this one's just watching," Scott explained, pointing first to the roadster, then to the bigger car in the foreground. Gary gave another little hug and smile.

"That's great. That one looks like it could go pretty fast," said Gary, pointing to the roadster.

"It can! It has flames on it!" Scott exclaimed, nodding his head in agreement. He put the paper back down on the board to put the finishing touches on the picture.

10-9 97_Scott_8

One of Scott's car drawings done later at age eight

Because he enjoyed playing outside he didn't watch a lot of television. He did, however, have one favorite show, *The Jetsons*. He was captivated by this cartoon set in the future, with flying cars and buildings that looked like little space stations. The main characters were a family of four including a boy named Elroy. Once, as I was returning from a trip I spotted a plastic Elroy Jetson doll in an airport store. It looked just like him—eight inches tall, in green tights, green long sleeved shirt with a wide yellow belt, and a pointy "space age" hat.

When I got home, I presented it to Scott. He took one look, promptly scowled and walked away, shoving it to the floor. He would have nothing to do with it. I tried giving it to him a couple more times, but he had the same reaction. So I tested it one more time, using a different tactic.

"Scotty, *The Jetsons* are on TV. Do you want to play with your Elroy doll?" I asked, sitting beside him, holding the doll.

"No! No dollies!" pushing the doll away. The doll never appeared again.

Since Scott was an active kid, I decided to introduce him to skiing, one of my favorite sports. He was almost four when I ventured to the mountain with him. I collected used equipment, bundled him up, and headed up to Purgatory in Durango, Colorado, forty miles from our home in Farmington. I thought I would be his teacher this first time, get him introduced, and enroll him in lessons later if he wanted to continue. I wasn't exactly sure how to proceed, though. I'd seen other parents do a variety of things, and decided to mimic a couple of their teaching methods. We began with Scott skiing between my legs, pushing his skis against mine while I just held on to him. He quickly got the hang of that, putting his skis in the snowplow, with tips of the skis together in a wedge position. We only spent a half day that first time.

Early ski practices in our backyard before I took him to the mountain.

The next time was a real adventure. We started out reviewing the position. Then he looked up at the chairlift.

"I want to go up there," he said excitedly, pointing up the mountain.

"You can't go up there until you learn how to turn," I said, making my words clear and deep for emphasis.

We worked on turning for most of the morning. It wasn't long before it seemed he was grasping the concept. There was a chair lift on the smaller "bunny hill" so I decided to chance it. I showed him how it worked and how to get on. He made it on all right, with the help of the attendant. He may have enjoyed the ride but I was a nervous wreck.

"Mommy, look!" he cried out as he scooted to the front of the chair pointing to the skiers below. I immediately put my arm out to push him back, trying to keep my nerves in check. My heart raced.

"You need to sit still while we're going up, Scott. Pull your bottom back against the chair," I gasped, pushing him farther back.

But he would have none of that. He started twisting and turning, trying to watch all the activity below him. "Wow! We're in the sky!" he exclaimed. He was fascinated by the tops of trees going by.

In those days, before the high-speed quad lifts, there was no safety bar on the slow-moving double chair. The seats would become very slippery in cold, wet weather. His every move set my nerves quivering.

We finally made it to the top. The slope wasn't that much steeper than we had been practicing on so I thought he would do OK. I held on to his jacket as we skied down together. He turned fairly well, with my prompting and direction, but he still had a propensity to go straight. We took another trip up the chair. Halfway down, I decided to see if he had actually learned anything. I let him go down a little hill, telling him he could go without me, and I would meet him at the bottom. Wide eyed and grinning, he took off. Bending his knees, getting into a tuck, with skis in wedge position, he was off. I let him get a head start before starting down a short way behind him. He was heading down the hill but directed toward the trees. Before I knew it, he was heading straight for the trees with no sign of turning. I raced down the hill, grabbing his jacket, to steer him out of harm's way. My heart pounded. I directed him into the chairlift line, still shaking from what might have been.

"Mommy! That was fun! Do it again!" he shouted as he looked up at me with eyes wide as could be and the biggest smile on his face.

Let's not! was my first thought.

"We can go up again but you have to *turn*, like we practiced," I told him, willing my heart rate back to normal.

Later I enrolled him in ski school, figuring they knew better how to teach little guys. However, after several weeks the instructor approached me.

"Scott has to learn how to follow directions," she said. "He's creating a problem because he wants to go on his own." Once again, he had demonstrated his aptitude for getting down the hill the fastest way possible. It also demonstrated his tendency for doing things his own way, regardless of what he was told.

It would prove to be another front in the war we would fight with him in the coming years. He took one more season of skiing lessons, then found other activities that held his interest. Although he didn't turn out to be my "ski buddy," later on in his teen years he got me into snowboarding and we did enjoy many exciting times on the slopes.

Taking a pastorate in Vancouver, WA as Scott came into school age, we debated about whether to homeschool, look for a private Christian school, or enroll in public school. The Christian school was out of our price range. I felt it would be best for an only child to be around other kids, to develop his social skills. Public school was OK by him, since all the other boys in the neighborhood went to the same elementary school.

I had heard frightful tales of early morning battles, of moms fighting with their kids to get up and get ready for school. I never had such a problem. I was amazed how early he could get up. After Gary and I had bedtime prayer with him, as part of our usual routine, I stayed to tuck him in the evening before the first day of school.

"I have to go to the store in the morning," I said, "but I'll be back to get you up for breakfast." I turned out the light just before going out the door of his bedroom.

"Mom," he asked, sitting up with a little glint in his eye. "Can I go with you?"

"I'll be going very early in the morning. Are you sure you want to get up that early?" I walked back over to the edge of the bed and leaned over. "I'll have to get you up at six o'clock so we can get back in time for breakfast and then catch the bus. Do you think you want to do that?" I wasn't trying to discourage him but I was hesitant. I wasn't sure of his motivation. Was it just to be with me? I'd like to think so. Was it something different? He definitely had an inclination for being different. That was certainly evident as he grew older. But for whatever reason, it gave me an indication of what he could do if he wanted to. He showed determination to do whatever it took to accomplish his desire. Foreshowing of things to come.

"OK, I will," he said, as he laid his head back down on the pillow. Pulling up the covers, I kissed him good night and left the room, still wondering what motivated him. *But we'll see if he really does this,* I thought.

Six o'clock came and I went into his room thoroughly expecting him to just roll over and go back to sleep when I awakened him.

I shook his shoulder slightly and whispered, "Hey, Bug. Time to get ready, if you still want to go shopping. Get your clothes on for school. I'll be ready in a couple of minutes."

"OK, Mom," he said sleepily. With no other prompting, he got up, put his clothes on, and met me out in the dining room ready to go. Sure enough, he had on his jeans, green Lego T-shirt, socks, and shoes. He put on his jean jacket and we were out the door.

During the hour or so that we were shopping we had great conversations about what we were shopping for, what he was going to do that day, and some things I had planned to do. I would give him an item to get if he was familiar with it. Most of the time he came back with the right thing. Sometimes he would ride in the cart and sometimes he would push. He would get a little carried away as he pushed, putting his head down and not paying attention to where he was going. I had to remind him to watch out for other carts and that this was not a racetrack. I had to chuckle, though, as it reminded me of his toddler days, recklessly pushing his stroller along the sidewalk in our neighborhood. That seemed like just yesterday. But it was all good. It turned out to be something I would look forward to. Who knew early-morning grocery shopping with my son could be enjoyable?

Scott was a real ham; age five

He had played soccer since age five and was quite good. He continued to play but was also showing an interest in skateboarding. Tony Hawk, the pro skateboarder, was hot. Scott watched all his videos and immediately tried to emulate all the moves. We immediately became immersed in the lingo of skateboarding—goofy foot, nosegrind, fakie—and Gary had to learn all about the wheels. Keeping them in good running order seemed like a full-time job. Scott was quick to master the basic tricks and soon became the talk of the neighborhood. We even set up a small rail and ramp in front of the house to practice. Oh, of course, he coaxed Mom into trying as well. I had done some of this earlier in my girlhood but things were very much different now, and I don't mean just the equipment. With those extra years, I wasn't feeling as confident as I remembered having been before.

Soccer days, age seven

"Come on, Mom, you can do it," Scott hollered back as he raced ahead of me. Just as I caught up with him, he did a heelside grind on the curb and looked back, expecting me to follow. Since just keeping upright at a reasonable pace was a chore, I opted out of the challenge. But I relished doing these activities with my son, who was the all-American boy.

He was definitely showing more artistic skill at this point, already able to draw much better than I! Recognizing his academic and art aptitudes, his third-grade teacher recommended an advanced placement program for the "gifted and talented." It would place more emphasis on the creative components of both academic learning and learning the diverse arts. However, it meant he would go to another school for part of the day.

We thought it good to start developing his interest. My father was a visual artist by trade and he always encouraged early development of art. There were certainly pros and cons. The next year Scott started what turned out to be three years of this program. It was an advantage that he did get exposure to the arts. However, he was splitting his time between two schools, spending two days a week at his "home" school and three days at the other school. He felt he was losing valuable time with his best friends. He didn't always know what was going on in the neighborhood when he would come back. Missing out on events that his friends were taking part in made him feel left out. Another issue made him feel left out—his allowance.

Unfortunately, this was during our family "economic downturn." We didn't have a lot to spend on extra things. All the other kids in the neighborhood were getting a pretty hefty allowance. We believed the allowance should be commensurate with work and responsibility. We didn't believe in giving him money just for being part of the family. Scott earned a meager allowance each week for simple chores completed. If he had something he really wanted, he would first ask us to buy it for him. If we said no, he knew it was up to him to save his allowance.

Since many times saving his allowance took too much time, he started gathering cans and bottles for recycling to get extra income. I would help from time to time, going to different parts of the neighborhood, looking for treasures tossed into bushes or left in the streets. Searching for one can at a time became tedious. We made an alternate plan.

"Mom, can I get cans out of the recycle bins on the curbs?" Scott asked.

"I do believe once they're on the curb they belong to the city," I answered, not totally sure. I hoped it would be enough to dissuade him from doing something wrong, if indeed, it was illegal to take things out of the bins. I didn't want to give him any loopholes. He was always one for circumventing the rules. His idea of rules was they were more like strong suggestions with leeway to bend them to accomplish his purpose. In this case, he reasoned since they were on a public street it was public domain. Unfortunately, his rationalization of rules would not serve him well in the future.

"What you might do, Scotty, is ask the people to save their cans and bottles for you and then collect them on recycling days," I suggested, relieved I had some positive alternative action.

"Yeah, I guess I could," he responded, nonchalantly. Several of the neighbors we asked were more than happy to save them for him. He then began to ask people in the church and people in other neighborhoods if they would do the same. Before too long he had quite a few customers.

I got curious as to what he was saving for. Christmas was coming and I knew there were a couple of items on his list that we weren't going to get him but that he really wanted.

"They have the Game Boy at the Toys R Us store, Mom. Will you take me down to get it? It's on sale the day after Thanksgiving," he asked with much anticipation.

"Good grief! We'd have to go at four o'clock in the morning! There's going to be a long line of people. Do you really want to stand out in the cold all that time?" I asked, knowing full well he would do almost anything for that precious item.

The Game Boy, a handheld video game, was the current craze with all the kids. He was the only one in his circle of friends who didn't have one. We had told him it was something he needed to buy with his money so he had saved diligently for it. Now he was jumping at the opportunity to get it at a bargain price.

I remembered our early-morning grocery shopping and knew he wouldn't have a problem. I, on the other hand, was not looking forward to getting up early, standing in line in the cold, and fighting the crowd once inside. It wasn't my idea of a nice rest after the Thanksgiving holiday. But since he was making the effort, I guessed I could suffer through it. So we did.

We got down to the store at about four o'clock and sure enough, the line was already long. It was a typical early winter morning but we dressed for it and endured the wait. Fortunately, it wasn't raining or drizzling as it most often did this time of year. Once inside it was as I anticipated—a giant Easter egg hunt for adults. Parents were running through the aisles, pausing just long enough to grab something off the shelves, and then hurrying to make sure they would secure the next item on the list before they were all gone. Scott knew exactly what he wanted—apparently lots of others wanted it, too. For security purposes, the store didn't put this item on the rack. You had to find the item's card, then take it to a separate counter to procure the actual item. When Scott found the necessary card, he grabbed it and started toward the counter.

"Hurry, take your card up to the counter and get it," I said, nudging and pointing him in the direction of the desk nearby. "There's lots of people up there, go get in line." My heart started beating faster as I anticipated what might happen if this long-awaited moment did not come to pass.

Staying back by the rack, I watched him run up to the line, excitedly holding the precious card. Straining to watch, I stayed in the background. Because of the Game Boy's popularity and the number of people waiting in line, I knew it would be close whether he would get one. I tried not to be anxious. I kept peering over the line of people, creeping a little closer to hear any conversation. I saw him finally getting to the counter and talking to the attendant. I didn't catch the exact words but he appeared to have told Scott there were no more left. Deciding to intervene, I pushed my way up to him.

I heard Scott say, almost in tears, "I've got a card for it. There *has* to be another one." Immediately my heart sank. *Oh, no, after all this, he missed it by that much?* A lump formed in my throat as I fought back tears.

The young clerk was very kind and seemed apologetic about the circumstances. However, as he saw the line behind Scott, he decided not to take any more time with him. Just then, an older, heavyset gentleman approached and the clerk explained the situation to him. I assumed he was a manager as he looked at Scott and said, "Let me see if we have any more in the back." He turned and disappeared into the rows of shelves behind him. We stepped aside to let the clerk service other customers.

I didn't know what to say to Scott. I was just as heartbroken as he was. His head and shoulders slumped, his mouth began quivering, and his eyes started to water. He looked so dejected. We both kept staring into that cavern of toys in the back, hoping upon hope that the dreamed-of item would appear. Coming through the shadows, the man reappeared. Straining over the counter, we tried to see if he had the prized piece in his hand.

"There was one left—you're lucky," he said, putting the treasured item in Scott's outreached hands. Again, my heart skipped a beat but this time for joy.

"Thanks!" Scott grasped the toy tightly, eyes now wide with excitement. When we reached the checkout counter, he carefully counted out his money, coin by coin. We both breathed a sigh of relief as we left the store; Scott because he finally got what he wanted and I because I had survived the early-morning madness of a "Black Friday" frenzy. I vowed never to repeat the adventure.

Although it was a harried experience for me, it proved to be valuable. I learned a lot about my son. His perseverance to reach a goal was amazing. It took a lot of determination to keep getting those cans week after week. Knowing that it was all on him to get what he wanted showed real fortitude. In the end, however, those same traits proved to be his undoing as he pursued another goal.

Chapter 2

COLLIDING WORLDS

To man belong the plans of the heart,
but from the Lord comes the reply of the tongue.
Proverbs 16:1

Scott was lying on his bed, propped up against the headboard, nose in his favorite book, *Calvin and Hobbs.* Peering into his room I paused for just a second, relishing the thought of just being his mom. His short, dark-blonde hair just a bit mussed; his longish nose, so much like his dad's, and his now-developing muscular body. I was thinking, *He's going to be the male image of the athletic me.*

Our relationship was something I treasured. We had a few bumps here and there, as to be expected, but overall we were close. In many ways he was my buddy, participating in activities with me that Gary wasn't able to do and some of my friends were not about to do! We skateboarded, snowboarded, played basketball with the neighbor boys, played tennis, and rode bikes. We even engaged in a little football with the guys. Summer evenings, other friends would drop by the house. The basketball hoop in front of the neighbors' house across the street held an invitation.

One evening several of the guys began shooting around. I was doing yard work so I wandered a little closer to the front yard to see the action. Without hesitation they asked if I would join them for a pickup game. When I said yes, I was immediately picked as the first member of Scott's team. That surprised me, but I assumed the choice was based largely on the fact I was Scott's mom. Later, I asked him what he thought about that, to make sure I wasn't embarrassing him. "Heck no, Mom, you're the best out there!"

We talked about a lot of things. When he saw me peeking into his room that day, and asked if he could ask me a question, I didn't think it out of the ordinary.

It started out innocently enough. Many tweens are grappling with changes in their bodies, their attitudes, life in general. I remember having lots of questions at that stage so I thought I could be of help as I certainly had "been there, done that." However, this particular day he asked the question that would change our relationship in many ways and cause our worlds to collide.

"Mom, did you ever think you should have been a boy?"

Oh, my, how many thoughts flooded my mind and memory, thoughts Scott couldn't have imagined that his question had triggered!

Chapter 3

MY EARLY YEARS

*I remember the days of long ago; I meditate on all your works
and consider what your hands have done.*
Psalm 143:5

COME ON! WE'VE been in here long enough. This seat is
hard. History is boring. The sun is shining. Please, can't you excuse
us just a little early? We only have forty-five minutes for recess!
Those were my thoughts as I sat at my desk, waiting for the
clock to tick off those last minutes before I could be outside
and play. Every minute outside was precious as I tried to pack
in as much activity as possible in those ever-fleeting moments.
My favorite was square ball. The ultimate challenge was to get
to be the server and then to stay, putting out as many chal-
lengers as possible while protecting one's position. I held my
own with the guys, beating many along the way. They got over

thinking of me as a girl when I started being one of the best players. I relished the fact that I didn't hit "like a girl" and could put a pretty good punch behind the ball. Every once in a while, I would look over at the clique of girls doing whatever they were doing and thinking I was having so much more fun than they were. I belonged with the guys, rather than trying to fit into a world of frills and small talk, a world I never felt I could ever be part of.

I have always liked to be in the middle of the action. My older brother was involved in sports so, being the little sister, I insisted that I be a part as well. To him I was just an annoying little sister who wanted to tag along.

"Jude, you can't go with us. We're going to play baseball. Stay here," my brother said as he pedaled off on his bike with his friends, bat and glove in hand.

"But I want to go, too," I said, pouting.

Dad was my biggest supporter. After explaining to me why I couldn't do "those things," he accommodated my desires by teaching me particular aspects of those sports, how to hit a ball with a bat, how to throw a baseball, how to throw a nice tight spiral with a football. He took me out to play tennis. Each day when he came home from work I would be eagerly waiting to see what we could do together. That's just one reason Dad and I were so close.

Although we shared family activities, such as skiing and camping, Mom and I never had that kind of relationship. As I started participating in all these sports, I thought Mom would embrace the idea, especially since she enjoyed these activities as well. But coming from a family that was distant with each other it was difficult for her to communicate her feelings in a warm and welcoming way. I never felt free to come to her with problems like I could with Dad.

My grandfather, Dad's dad, had to overcome his preconceived idea about what I should do as a girl. Grandpa wanted a princess and although he never expressed his disappointment at having a tomboy, I rather suspected it. Every year when the Rose Festival would come around, he would look at me and wink, implying, *Someday you'll be one of those princesses.* Dad, though, always encouraged me to do what I liked to do, whether anybody else was doing it or not. I've never forgotten the words that he said to us so often, "You can be anything you want to be." Those words have carried me through a lot of tough times.

But then as I grew older, I got the impression I was engaging in activities that girls weren't supposed to do. I liked climbing trees, playing in the dirt, riding my bike over rough and bumpy roads, and playing ball sports. I started to wonder, *What **are** girls supposed to do?* I had played dolls with some of my girlfriends and that was OK but as soon as something better came along I was out the door. Dresses were something I put up with, especially during those early years where we had to wear them to school, church, or any other social event. I put them on when I had to and generally took pants along to change into whenever I could. So in those ways I acquiesced to a "girl's world." But most of all, I enjoyed the empowerment of moving my body to accomplish things athletically. I wanted to challenge myself physically, to compete, and the guys allowed me to do that.

I don't want to give the impression that I was unbeatable at this stage. Oh, I certainly wanted to be. We had "field days" in grade school—the closest thing to a track meet for girls in those days. I was the best at our school. However, in events with the other two schools in town, I realized I was not the fleetest of foot. So I did have competition.

Junior high years are tumultuous. You're trying to figure out who you are, what the world is about, how you fit in, so that world is pretty much centered on you. When I entered junior high from elementary school, I lost my playtime. What would I do during lunch break? I was used to being with my friends, the guys, playing games on the playground. Now all of a sudden everything was different—something drastic had happened during that summer. I felt as if I had been left behind somewhere along the line or had missed the instructions on how to be a "girlfriend" to these guys.

To say I was lost is an understatement! I secretly wished I were a boy because they could go and play sports and run around and do things they had always been doing. Girls, on the other hand, had to act like girls. I had no clue as to what that was supposed to entail. I stood on the steps of the school that first day and wondered, *Where do I go from here?*

There was no question in my mind that I was a girl. God created me one, so I accepted that as fact. I knew not to question God's sovereignty. Christianity was a major part of our family structure.

Being raised in a Christian home I took for granted that we went to church every Sunday and didn't do those things Christians aren't supposed to do, like swear, drink, or gamble. I thought I was a Christian because I had been raised in a Christian household, and had Christian parents.

It was the summer after fifth grade. I didn't especially like the church my parents were attending so I started attending church with my best friend. When she invited me to go to camp, I was thrilled! I had never been to a church camp before. Everything was exciting—the Bible stories, the Kool-Aid at meals, and especially the pool and recreation time. There were contests between cabins and prizes awarded to special campers. Listening to the speaker, however, was a challenge. We had to sit still for a whole thirty minutes. What a stretch! My mind wandered to the games we had played and the contest we would do next. But this time there was a missionary doctor speaking. I found myself listening for two reasons—number one, he was a doctor and I was totally interested in doctor things, and number two he said we were all sinners.

He emphasized the "all" coming from the reference in Romans 3:23: "All have sinned and fallen short of the glory of God." There were no exceptions or qualifications. He went on to explain that if that's true then we are all sinners. Then he cited Romans 6:23, which said that the consequence of being a sinner was death; he explained this was eternal separation from God. Wow! That got my attention, since I thought my relationship with God was totally good because of who I was in my family. But he explained further that the rest of that verse is the best part, that God has a free gift for us, eternal life with Him. I had never thought of it that way. If we wanted to receive that free gift and have a personal relationship with Jesus, we could accept what Jesus did on the cross in paying for our sins; that is, He died and took the death penalty for me so I didn't have to. He talked about Jesus rising from the dead and being alive for us so we could be the person He created us to be. Then he quoted John 3:16 (which I had heard many times before) in a very unique way. "For God so loved the world"—then he paused and told us to put our name silently in place of "the world." *Wow*, I thought, *that's really personal. God really loves me.* So I said, "Judy," silently to myself. Then he continued, "that He gave His only begotten Son that whosoever"—he paused again and told us to put our name in place of "whosoever." Again, I said, "Judy," silently inside. Then he finished, "believes in Him should not perish but have everlasting life." At that point I realized I had never made that decision before. I took that step, believed in Jesus Christ and His work as my only way to God. I knew that I had that everlasting relationship with Him. I have never doubted since.

Now during those confusing days in junior high the words "being the person He created me to be" came back to my mind. What kind of person did He create me to be?

It was around this time that the powers-that-be in our school started to think that junior high girls could handle more organized sports, like basketball. But I guess "they" figured that we poor feminine creatures would either die of total exhaustion or start growing hair on our chest if we ran too far, that is, the full length of the basketball court. You could have one "rover" who could cross the center line and go full court but woe to the other five players who dared touch their toe on that precarious barrier, that center line, separating the two teams. These folks also figured we weren't coordinated enough to run and bounce the ball at the same time so we could only dribble three times before having to get rid of the ball. Fortunately, I was usually the roving player so I didn't go stir crazy watching the game from the other side.

Organized sports fed the hungry monster in me that was beginning to have an insatiable appetite. It felt so good to be able to play, compete, and do it against other girls. I couldn't get enough of playing sports and being competitive. For the first time we were able to be a real team with a coach who told us how to do things that would make us better. Awesome! Oops—one drawback. Girls couldn't be highly competitive *and* be feminine *and* popular with the boys. Where did that leave me? On a teeter totter trying to balance the basketball that I enjoyed, and wanting this new attitude with the boys that I hadn't quite figured out yet.

One day I came up with a brilliant idea. I would go out for cheerleading! I would still play basketball but by becoming a cheerleader I would gain necessary popularity because everyone knows cheerleaders are popular.

The cheer required for tryouts wasn't difficult. I practiced all the neat little moves in front of my mirror. I made sure my voice could be heard in the next county. Visions of accolades danced in my head. I was going to be surrounded by myriads of adoring fans.

On the day of the tryouts, the student council, teachers, and all the other candidates sat in the bleachers waiting as I was called to perform my little ditty. I wore my cutest blouse, brightly printed full skirt, matching vest, and saddle shoes. I thought I was all prepared. That is, until I stood in center court with my peers and teachers staring intently, waiting for me to begin. I would have felt more comfortable on the free-throw line waiting to shoot the ball and break a tied basketball game with one second left. What little self-confidence I had gathered in my practice time in front of the mirror left me. I was awkward and self-conscious. *What am I doing up here?* I asked myself. *Oh, well, might as well go through with it.* In the middle of the routine I realized this was like an elephant trying out for the New York City Ballet! My neatly tucked-in blouse was no longer tucked, my full skirt was getting in the way, and my shoes weighed a ton, so I was lucky to get off the ground when I jumped. My feeble voice barely reached the front row of bleachers. As the polite applause faded, I sat down, my thoughts ranging from *What a fool!* to *At least I can say I did it once.* But it took no hard urging to convince me cheerleading was not my niche. Afterward, walking toward the gym door, I knew I had just made the biggest and most embarrassing mistake of my life. Fortunately, no one mentioned it the following days. After that experience, I was more adamant than ever that I would stick to running up and down the court and *they* could run up and down the sidelines.

But the one sport I always liked most was football. I played any chance I could get, from just playing catch with Dad to joining in a pickup game with some guys at the park. It so happened that football became another mile marker along my journey to discovering that person who God created me to be.

Obviously there was no football for girls in high school. But I still didn't see why we couldn't play it. So I took matters into my own hands. Since they had "Powder Puff" this-and-that I figured we could have a "Powder Puff" football game. I got together with some of the other girls on the basketball team and we decided that we could have a game between the junior and senior girls. We cleared it with the higher powers and it was on. I was ecstatic. Imagine! Playing in a real football game! We got some of the guys from the football team to do the coaching and we were off and running-literally.

Selection of the positions was another matter. Well, surely I would be the quarterback because of my expertise in handling the football. Wrong. Not that I couldn't handle the football—that was no problem. The problem was at the other end. Apparently I threw the ball too hard for the receivers to catch. I was disappointed until the coach assigned me to a running back position so that was OK.

We drew a crowd for our inaugural event. It was at the end of the regular football season. It was a great feeling just being on the field and seeing people in the stands watching us. Although my team didn't win, I felt triumphant in the fact that everyone seemed to enjoy it. The game between the junior and senior girls became an annual event for several years.

Taking on the girls' football event gave me a sense of accomplishment. I was exhilarated. It wasn't so much that I had played football, as it was that for the first time I had done something against the grain and had survived. I not only survived, I thrived. I also maintained my femininity. No hair sprouted on my chest, my voice didn't deepen, and I could put on a dress the next day for church and look feminine. The lesson from that event would later play a major role in my life.

Throughout junior and senior high school, I was part of a very supportive and loving youth group. We were all close during those years, doing many activities together. They accepted me as I was, a tomboy "athletically inclined." When I was a sophomore, one of the guys, a senior at the time, started to take an interest in me. We had done some work on a friend's farm, moving pipe, bucking hay, and doing odd jobs that were considered heavy-duty manual labor. We worked alongside each other. He understood what I was like and what I liked to do. Eventually this boy from the church and I established a dating relationship.

Our church group had invited another church over for a Sunday afternoon of activities at the park and then an evening of singing. It was one of those perfect fall days that had the smell of football in the air. The group succumbed to the call. The boys promptly chose up their teams while the girls picked their spots on the sidelines. Our team came up short a player so one of the fellows asked if I wanted to play. Only slightly jesting, "Oh, you want *me* to play?" I ran on the field. I was in seventh heaven. Once again I was mixing it up with the boys. I loved the fact that I could hold my own and play respectfully and several of the guys commented on my abilities. One did not.

After the game, my boyfriend took me aside and told me it was "either me or football." I was dumbfounded. My mouth must have gotten tangled up in my shoelaces because I couldn't say a word. He said nothing more. There weren't exactly icicles between us but there was mighty heavy frost. I didn't understand this attitude as he had no trouble with me working in the hay field bucking fifty- to sixty-pound hay bales with the other guys. Why should this bother him?

Didn't he accept me for who and what I was? Would I have to be somebody I wasn't in order to keep his affection? Would I ever be able to enjoy these talents freely that I felt I had? Would there ever be someone out there who would let me be me—the person God created me to be, with these athletic gifts and desires?

I continued to enjoy all the sports in high school, including our annual junior-senior football game. After several years dating this guy, I realized he was not the one I wanted to spend my life with. I was now in college, which opened up a whole new vista of athletics. I *really* found out I was a little fish in a big pond. That bigger pool of athletic talent made me strive all the more and I flourished in my physical education major. However, a "coincidental" meeting with another athlete would change the course of my athletic career.

I had become involved with Campus Crusade for Christ through a friend involved with the organization. She suggested I work at the California headquarters as summer staff.

Now being a summer staff member at the headquarters meant you were part of the part-time *maintenance* staff. Full-time staff were required to assemble for further training in evangelism and Bible studies. However, the summer staff were allowed to sit in on classes. It was an awesome experience, to take in classes and speakers without having to do the homework. The downside for me, though, was being assigned to the housekeeping crew, as housecleaning was not my thing. Since one of my regular cleaning areas was the training room, one of my fellow crew members asked if I wouldn't mind asking the head of the weightlifting team if she and some others could use the training room for an exercise class. I told her I would be glad to do that, though, I had no idea whom I should talk to. I picked a time to go when I thought I might find someone in charge. When I got to the weight room, there was only one member of the team there casually working out since the full-time staff was attending a meeting.

This room was filled with iron bars, heavy metal plates, and chalk strewn over the lifting platform. Since I cleaned only the bathrooms and tidied up the outside, I hadn't really been inside the room. Once inside, I found it intimidating. Before me was this muscular man lifting a massive weight on the bench press. His grunts indicated he was obviously working very hard and concentrating on the task at hand, so I hung back until he finished. Wondering whether or not to approach him, I debated if I should interrupt him or wait until he noticed me. I felt as though I was invading a sanctuary and started to doubt if I should even be there. I summoned up courage and slowly walked over to him as he sat on the bench, wiping his head.

"Excuse me, could you tell me where I could find the person in charge?" I asked timidly.

"Oh, he's not here. There was an accident with his friend's little boy—he's at the hospital with him," he answered as he stood up from the bench.

Putting his shirt on, he continued. "He might be back but I couldn't tell you when. Could I help you with anything?"

A little intimidated by this quite muscular fellow, I said the only thing that came to mind, "No, I'll just wait." I stepped outside and sat down on a chair, looking at the wonderfully lit sky.

After a few minutes, he came over to me, pulled up a chair, and he introduced himself as Gary. Because the team had been introduced at an earlier all-staff meeting, I knew he was the only single team member. Being the only unmarried member of the weightlifting team and a very well-built specimen, I knew he had his choice of available girls. That he paid any attention to me was quite surprising. As we chatted I became rather smitten with this fellow. He proceeded to tell me about himself, where he was from, the schools he had attended, his family, and then a little about the team. Then, before we parted, he offered to show me some things about weight training. I was shocked. *Really? You would do that?* I showed restraint in my answer, as I didn't want to appear too eager. But my head was spinning with excitement! I had always wanted to lift weights but had been told that it was something "girls shouldn't do." I had no idea that meeting would change my life forever.

I did go back to meet him at the arranged time and he introduced me to some weight training exercises. I was totally enthralled and excited about this new adventure. I loved testing my strength and eagerly engaged in whatever he told me to do. I was surprised that a guy would actually encourage this. This definitely was not something a girl normally did. I became "bitten by the iron bug" and couldn't get enough. In the back of my mind I thought how wonderful it would be to really get to know this guy romantically, but I knew I was up against some stiff competition. There were a lot of single women at this place much more feminine, experienced, older, and smarter than I. I didn't feel I had much to bring to the table as far as a romantic interest.

By the time I had to go back to college for my senior year we had become pretty well-acquainted. Since I had become so enthralled with weightlifting, I tried to duplicate the training regimen he set up. However, I didn't have access to equipment so I didn't make much progress. I was more involved with sports but did what I could with what little equipment I had. Gary came to visit me at school that October and we had a chance to get reacquainted. I showed him what I was able to do with the weights and he was pretty excited about it. We wrote back and forth through the fall. He was occupying my thoughts more and more and I thought a long-term commitment was possible. I couldn't quite read his intent at this time, but I was getting the impression he was going that direction as well. At Christmas, he invited me to fly back to Pennsylvania to meet his family. Seems my impression was correct and the relationship was moving forward. I finished my senior year and that summer he invited me to drive out to California with him from his parents' home in Pennsylvania. I flew out and spent a day or two with his parents before we loaded up his '69 Volkswagen with my little bag and his few belongings and headed out west.

It was quite a trip. Not wanting to spend the money on two rooms at a motel, we opted for driving as far as possible before becoming totally tired. We stopped to sleep where we could. One night we spent on a park table. Another night we spent on the lawn of a well-populated public park. It was exciting for me but nerve wracking for Gary, since he always slept with one eye open anticipating trouble. Upon arriving in California, we checked in at our appropriate places- he in regular staff housing and I in the new staff housing, as I had been accepted as a member of full-time staff. We quickly settled into our own routines. Although we hadn't talked much about it, I had a feeling marriage was on the horizon. It wasn't long afterward that he proposed and we became engaged on Father's Day. Because the weightlifting team's schedule had already been set, we had to work a wedding date around that. We were married nine weeks after he proposed. It was a marriage forged in steel since weightlifting was a part of both our lives as members of the weightlifting team. I couldn't believe how God had answered my prayer in giving me a guy who actually encouraged me to do something I enjoyed that was not only athletic but totally off the feminine radar. Yes, we were joined in our common passion of weightlifting, but another passion was troubling me.

I entered into this marriage with a nagging fear. I wasn't like other women. I had a hard time being "flirty" and wondered if I could be sexually alluring to my husband. I felt more comfortable in a sweat suit hitting a ball than I did in a flimsy negligee. I had these thoughts before we were married but now on our honeymoon suddenly, I felt very awkward. The same feelings I had experienced during cheerleading tryouts came back to me. *What am I doing?* Except now I had a husband to perform for. *What is he going to think? Will he have any doubts about me?* As I tried my best to put on the sexy act that I felt was expected, I realized all too quickly how different I must be. What was wrong with me? Those fears would have been confirmed had I known at the time about a conversation between

Gary and my dad; Dad had asked him how serious he was about me. "Serious," Gary related he had said, and Dad replied, "You know, she's not like other girls."

Through the years, I discovered there was nothing wrong with me. It was who I am—the package God put together to make me who I am. He brought me the right man who would understand and accept, even embrace, that I *was* different from other women. Recognizing God's unconditional love for me, I finally accepted myself. Gary was amazing in showing me how much he loved me, too. I knew God would work in Scott's life as well, if he would let Him. That was the biggest question— would Scott do that?

A lot of my old feelings resurfaced when my son asked me that painful question, "Mom, have you ever wanted to be a boy?" Where could the conversation start? At what point in this whole story could I begin to tell him that it was OK to wonder, to question, to feel insecure where he was right now? Scott knew what I had done in weightlifting, and he was certainly aware we shared many activities unusual for a mother and son to share. He knew I was different from other moms. But he didn't know about my struggles getting to this point in *my* life.

I was at a loss about how to convey the battle that raged in my own head; of feeling I should act and be something different than I was. I was hoping by the end of the conversation, or through succeeding conversations, I could help him sort things out. Oh, how I wished someone had come alongside *me* and helped me with *my* confused emotions at that time.

Little did I know that this little struggle would not have a quick resolution.

Chapter 4

ENTERING TWO WORLDS

Has reason disappeared?
And, God, are you near?
Suzy Kassen

With a slight smile I thought, *I know exactly how you feel. We'll talk about this and it will all be OK.* My mind went back to those times when I wondered why I liked the things I did; climbing trees, throwing balls, getting dirty, and so many other things girls aren't "supposed" to like. I was conflicted about what I wanted to be and do and other's expectations. So I knew exactly where Scott was coming from. I emphasized these things to him in hopes that he knew I understood. I didn't fit the norm but it was OK. I had gone ahead to do "my own thing" and it had worked very well. I thought I had put to rest any doubts he may have had about his own gender with my explanation of what had happened in my own life and encouraged him to do whatever he wanted. However, deep down, my heart told me something different with his response.

"I'm really a girl," he said as he looked up at me, rather casually. He crossed his legs, picked up his stuffed tiger, and started fiddling with it. Still lying restfully on his bed, he apparently didn't think this a big deal.

"Oh?" I questioned. I had to gather myself and think a second before responding. My heart was now pounding and my head was whirling. I broke out in a cold sweat.

Trying not to show my shock, and trying to convince myself discussion would dismiss his thought, I gave him a little smile and started to walk out the door. "Well, think some more about it and we'll talk about it," I finally said.

"Not anything to talk about," I heard him say quietly.

I wasn't prepared for this. How did this happen? Did I miss the signs along the way? This just didn't happen to Christians. We had given Scott all the "talks"; the drug talk, the sex talk, the "choose your friends wisely" talk. We had our bases covered. Maybe this was just a rough patch of questioning that every teen goes through.

For the most part Scott had been a good kid, not getting involved in the "bad stuff." We knew his friends, all pretty good kids. Late nights weren't generally a problem and he kept us in touch about his whereabouts. Not that he was perfect—far from it.

Scott and Gary at Disney World, our last big vacation together.
Scott was about eleven

But *this* situation was *totally* not in my playbook. It startled me so much I had to catch my breath. I knew nothing about this condition; I just knew there was no way he was supposed to be a girl. God had created him a male in both mind and body. His behavior had exhibited all the characteristics of maleness all through his early years. *What is going through his mind? If he really gets serious about this, how do I handle this? What will happen from here?* Lots of questions, no immediate answers. My first prayer was one of desperation, as so many pray when in a dire situation. ***Oh, God, help!*** Then, of course, I expected He would answer my prayer and deliverance would be forthcoming. There would be miraculous people showing up to give me all the wise counsel I needed. Thoughts would implant themselves in my brain to give me wonderful insights to his needs.

Signs and wonders of all sorts were just on the horizon to get me through this unexpected turn of events. *Well, maybe these miracles happened to others but it sure wasn't happening here.* Instead, I had to take one hard step at a time.

My first step was finding a counselor. This someone would certainly get to the root of the matter, make a few adjustments in Scott's attitude, and the problem would just go away. That was my plan and I expected it be God's plan as well.

So I approached Scott about getting help.

"Would you be willing to get counseling?" I asked matter of factly.

"I guess. But it can't be a *Christian* counselor," he replied with sarcasm.

"OK," I responded hesitantly. As I gave my weak assent to his request, I thought, *I'm not willing to entrust him to anyone who might undermine all the spiritual training we have given him these past years.* I think both Scott and I knew, tacitly, that a non-Christian counselor really wasn't going to happen. We had discussed our viewpoint and our biblical understanding, so he knew where we stood. He knew us well enough to figure that out. We left it at that and parted.

Our family at the beginning of Scott's counseling

But there was another matter. Scott started getting into something that completely shocked me. He became involved in the "Furry" culture, assuming the personality of a cat and took the name Pookey.

Shortly after we moved to Vancouver we acquired Friskey (a female) and Pookey (a male). Scott, about six years old at the time, took to them immediately, as he had to our two previous cats in New Mexico. He particularly latched onto Pookey. I couldn't quite figure out why Scott was so captivated by him. Maybe because he was the *most* independent and the *bossiest* cat we've ever had, a yellow and white tabby that ruled the neighborhood. Should another cat dare enter his territory, that is, his yard and several of the other yards adjacent, he would let them know who was king. On sunny days he would sit on the driveway like the proverbial monarch watching over his kingdom.

Most of his days he spent outdoors, ears perking and eyes darting toward any noise within earshot. When he did come inside he would put up with Friskey, letting her know she was merely tolerated in his presence. He would look at her with glaring eyes, signaling the king was present and she had better submit.

Oh, he would have his moments of affection but only when he wanted. You and your lap were merely another object to be used upon his majesty's request. He would walk up, look you affectionately in the eye, and demand you pet him as he curled on your lap. As he purred, he accepted your adoration. When he was finished he'd give a low growl and jump off. Yes, everything was on his terms.

Scott, now in his teens, would sign his drawings with the name, Pookey.

"Hey, Scott—what's with the Pookey name?" I asked, the first time I noticed.

"Pookey? He's rad. I wish *I* was a cat. They're the coolest animals," he explained with a glint in his eye.

"I know why *I* like cats but why do you?" I pushed for more explanation.

"I don't know. They're just cool, especially the big cats like tigers and lions. They got control and they know they're the best," he said. I sensed wistfulness in his voice.

Scott and Pookey

From that point on I became increasingly aware of his drawings of cats. He would personify them. He would draw them in human poses, but definitely with a cat's body and human emotions on their faces. Eventually I discovered he was being drawn into the Furry culture, something he had found online and pursued with people locally. People adopt a particular animal as their own character. Scott adopted a tiger as his character, blue and white as his colors. He would go to "Fur-Cons" and wear clothing representative of some aspect of the tiger, wearing arm coverings with blue stripes, hand coverings for legs and paws, and a tail as well. Hats or headbands always had ears. As time passed he would use his pseudonym more and more, drawing his character with the emotion he wanted to portray. Now well into his teens, two worlds were merging into one as he depicted himself as a blue and white, female tiger. I would see these drawings inadvertently every once in a while, drawn on school notebooks, or doodled onto papers he had left laying around. His tiger character would be smiling and jumping with excitement, with a caption: "See, I said I could do it!" Or it might be sitting down, head between knees, an obvious tear falling to the ground with the caption, "That really hurt me."

"Anime" became very popular at this time and he used its features consistently in depictions, especially big, round eyes. I could tell exactly what he was feeling just by looking at the picture. Since he wasn't freely expressing himself to us, I appreciated these glimpses into his emotions. But I didn't know what to think. I could not wrap my head around where *his* head was. I was scared. *What kind of world is he living in? What is luring him into this fantasy of now being an animal? Who does he think he is? Oh, Lord, what else is he getting into?*

Yet these detailed depictions showed the talent Scott had as an artist. As time passed I could see the development of this character and the many ways he was using it. He always had his sketch pad with him, filling several with only these drawings. He kept them private unless he would show me one he was especially proud of. These depictions made me all the more concerned that he was now creating two identities, losing touch from who he was as a person. I thought, *Does he really think he is a female cat?* I figured tackling both identities would be too much, so I decided I would try just to tackle the transgender condition, about which I knew next to nothing. Where in the world would I start?

Illustration of Pookey

Chapter 5

FINDING COUNSELING

Listen to counsel and accept discipline,
That you may be wise the rest of your days.
Many are the plans in a man's heart,
But the counsel of the Lord, it will stand.
Proverbs 19:20,21 (NASB)

As my journey to seeking help began, I didn't know where to go, who I was looking for, or what I was looking for. Should I call a psychiatrist? I didn't feel comfortable with a psychiatrist, knowing the background and training most have, so I didn't look there. How about a psychologist? Or maybe just a counselor in general? As I looked at website after website I discovered that these professions did not deal with the transgender issue. There were many who dealt with homosexuality but this was something totally different. After much searching I found a young counselor, Damon, who addressed teen sexual issues. His website mentioned a Christian background. He was not associated with any church or Christian organization. I figured, "close enough." When I asked about our specific problem he said he wasn't that familiar with the issue but would be willing to talk with Scott. I mentioned Scott's stipulation that the counselor not be Christian; Damon said he would comply and not play the Christian card, so to speak. Being the perceptive kid that Scott was, he didn't take long to figure out "where Damon was coming from." He mentioned it to me but didn't make a big deal about it. However, after several sessions, Damon told me Scott was no longer willing to open up and discuss several issues. Because of confidentiality he was not at liberty to say what those were. But by this time, it was getting toward the end of summer. Scott made an announcement after the last meeting. We got in the car and started home. Scott settled back in his seat.

"Hey, Mom?" Scott asked, getting my attention.

"Yes, I'm listening," I replied as I kept my eyes on the road.

"I don't think I'm going back to Damon anymore."

"Why not?" I asked, trying not to sound disappointed.

"School's starting pretty soon so I don't think I'll have much time for it." He started shifting, putting his feet on the dashboard, eyes forward, not looking at me.

"Oh, I think we can fit it in your schedule." I was desperate to keep this thing going. It was my only hope.

"No, I don't think so." I wasn't going to gain anything by forcing the issue.

There was a time gap between that step and the next. Scott was now in high school. He was getting into art more, taking classes at school and at a local art academy. He drew more cartoon characters and female cats.

Little battles were now cropping up. He wanted to let his hair grow out, an issue for both the school and his dad. We had always kept it short and he was fine with that up until now. Vancouver Christian High, where he was now attending, established that all the boys' hair was above their shirt collar. Dad wanted it shorter. Dad compromised to go with the school's policy. Of course Scott saw it "as close to the collar without touching." So it was.

Clothes were among those skirmishes. Very baggy pants with holes were Scott's preferred dress. He also liked oversized sweatshirts. This rubbed against Dad's sense of suitable attire. But we figured we had a bigger conflict to deal with so that, too, went by the wayside.

Scott spent two years at the Christian high school. Then he brought up the issue of schools.

"What would you say to me going to the public high school next year?" he inquired.

"Why?" was our logical response.

"I've never been with Joel or my other friends since grade school and I'd like to be with them for my last two years. Besides, there are more activities and more options for classes," he said, strongly presenting his case. Joel had been his best friend since he was five. I could see his point.

"We'll have to think about it," I answered.

After much discussion we did allow him to go to the public high school. As we reflect back, we suspect that "more activities" he mentioned were LGBT groups. But we didn't know that at the time.

At the end of that summer, just before his junior year, he started making overt gestures to his transition. We were hoping against hope that it was a passing thing. His hair was getting longer, almost touching his shoulders, and he started sewing clothes. He was very creative at this venture, I must say. He wanted oversized pants anyway, so he would take old jeans, cut out a section of the pant legs and make an insert to go into the pants he was wearing. He made a pair of bell-bottom jeans. He liked sewing and became adept at using my machine. He even remarked in passing about becoming a fashion designer. Since he had already made some items for his "Pookey" costume I thought that in the realm of possibility.

His next endeavor was to make a pair of pants out of duct tape, which he almost finished. He started out OK but then it became more difficult than anticipated. He brought Joel in on the project. I became curious about Scott's impromptu fashion debut.

"Hey, guys," I mentioned casually as the ever-encouraging mother. "Don't you think you need a pattern for this project?"

"Why? I'll be the model—no problem," Scott replied with no shortage of confidence.

"Well, it still would be a good idea to have *something* to go by if nothing but a box about your size to start wrapping it around," I said, still trying to convince them they needed a bit more planning.

"Mom, it can't be that hard. You got the top and two pant legs. We'll have it done in no time. They'll be so totally cool! I think I'll wear 'em to school," he said as he picked up the first of several rolls of gray duct tape.

It was going to be a simple enough project that they thought they could just go "by the seat of their pants," to use an old expression, pun intended! So he and Joel set out to create this wearable art. They started with the waistband. Scott wrapped tape around Joel's outstretched hands in a circle, which turned out way too big. Without trying it on they continued. They knew the hips needed to be a bit wider so Joel stuck his hands out, wider underneath the waistband, to give the hip a little flair. They would tape pieces vertically from the waistband for a "framework," then wrap around those pieces in the shape they wanted. Well, they certainly had flair. Of course the pants had no fly so they needed to make the waist and hip area big enough to just pull up. By this time they had gone through many rolls of tape; it was several layers thick and they were just beginning.

This garment, loosely termed, looked like a skirt. They taped up a little extra in the middle and made a crotch area, then tackled the legs. Each leg started out about six inches, attached at the hip. They decided that each would make a leg and attach it to the part he had started. By then they had spent several days on this thing. Joel, never one for lengthy projects, started getting tired. But Scott spurred him on to get his part of the leg done. Since it was getting to be expensive and interest was fading fast, neither leg got totally finished. Scott did attach his pant leg and discovered both he and Joel probably could have fit in it. Besides that, the pants were hot and totally inflexible. But by my standards, it was a valiant effort.

However, things were now starting to ramp up with Scott; there was more evidence of his effort to transition. Even in my state of denial I could see that. But I didn't want to admit to seeing what was in front of me: the longer hair, the drawings, the nail polish. I had no idea how to handle these issues, but I knew that something needed to be addressed. So I went back to my search for someone that Scott might be able to relate to. He had told me he *might* be open to talking with someone, but only upon his approval. I had to act while he was willing.

As an adjunct to his pastoring, Gary taught math in the evening at Clark College, where I also taught part time. During his time at school, Scott and I often took advantage of this time to talk. It was during one of those evenings that Scott asked me to come into his room. He was lying on the bed as I came in. Nothing seemed out of the ordinary. Then the bomb was dropped.

"Mom, I know I should have been a girl, so I am transitioning," he told me. "I can't hide it any more. I'm tired of pretending to be something I'm not."

Bang! The words struck me like a bombshell. *What? Really? No, you're not, and you* **know** *it!* I knew I couldn't speak those thoughts aloud as they went through my head. Feeling my legs getting weak, I sat down on the bed, my head whirling with reactions. I collected myself, and answered as calmly as I could.

"Why are you making this change? By genetics you're all male."

"I may be, by genetics, but my head tells me I'm a woman. I don't know any other way to put it."

"How long have you known this?"

"Since junior high. Remember how I liked to wear that Cat in the Hat hat that was really long? I liked to pretend I had long hair. I liked how it fell at my shoulders."

I shifted my position on the bed to squarely face him. Our eyes met only briefly. Bringing his legs up to his chest, he hugged his knees and put his head down. Still not looking at me he continued.

"You and Dad wouldn't understand. That's why I didn't tell you before. I knew you'd just flip out and go all berserk."

"So, where do we go from here?" I asked, desperately trying to hold on to whatever sanity I had left at this point.

"I don't know what *you're* going to do but I know what I have to do," he answered with a look of a quiet disdain mixed with sadness.

As he lay there on his bed I slowly scanned the walls of his room. Every single square inch of his four walls had something stuck or pasted on it: clippings from magazines of old cars, fast food pictures, pictures of himself with his buddies, patriotic scenes of flags and freedom sayings, images of skateboarders and snowboarders, outdoor scenes of mountains, pictures of cats he had drawn and cute animal photos he had cut out, bumper stickers and license plates he had collected. A thousand and one random things; one giant collage of who he was.

When I looked back at him, the feeling I got from him was mixed. I saw a little "please accept me and love me" with "I don't give a damn what you think because you're not going to like it anyway, so leave me alone." That minute that I stood there after our conversation looking at him seemed like forever.

My first impulse was to take him in my arms, hug him close and say, "It's Ok, we'll get through this." But then I realized this was not something we would just "get through." He was making a life-changing decision that would affect him forever, as well as us. It was also something we could not condone. So in his mind "getting him through this" would be to help him change, but in my mind "getting through this" would be, as it had been all along, to help him understand what this was all about *and* change his thinking. I also remember thinking, *This can't be! We were getting counseling and the problem was supposed to get better! How am I going to deal with this?!* After that long, uncomfortable pause I gave him a little hug. He snickered as he got up and walked out of the room.

I went to the gym, thinking I could get my mind off the problem. But I couldn't, and the more I thought about it, the more scared I got. I had to let it out. I felt I might explode if I didn't talk to somebody. I called my sister-in-law, my confidant in matters of the heart, and asked if I could come over. I said nothing about it over the phone so she suspected nothing. When I arrived at the house moments later, she greeted me in her usual loving, upbeat fashion.

"Hi, come on in. What's up?" She opened the door and gestured for me to enter the living room. Smiling as we both walked over to sit down, she was anticipating some wonderful news. What she got was quite the opposite.

I plopped down in the chair and immediately started crying, "Oh, Katie, Scott's going to be a woman!" I cried, sobbing uncontrollably. As my shoulders slumped down, I couldn't hold back my raw emotions of despair, confusion, and dashed hopes and dreams. "He just told me tonight he's making the transition. I don't know what to do." As she knelt down beside me and squeezed my hand, her countenance showed surprise, bewilderment, questioning. I looked into her eyes, searching for comfort, hope, answers, not sure what I was looking for.

"Oh, Jude, did you see this coming?" Her question was searching for some explanation.

"We've been going to counselors and I thought we were doing some good. He had questions about it but now his mind's made up. I don't know what to do!" I was trying to answer between sobs.

How could I explain to her all that had gone on the last several months? We had kept this under wraps, thinking it would be a temporary thing. She looked at me with questioning eyes, trying to comprehend what she had just heard. Then my brother came into the room. He had been busy in the garage and had just finished washing his hands.

"Oh, I didn't know you were here," he remarked as he noticed me in the chair. "Scott thinks he's a woman," Katie said softly. Then he, too, looked very concerned as he slumped into the chair beside me. The three of us just sat silent for what seemed like hours; none of us knowing just what to say.

"I don't know what to tell you except that we will pray for all of you. You know we're here for you if you just want to talk or cry or vent in any way," she finally said. "Anytime, day or night, even in the middle of the night," she continued. It wasn't a solution but it was a comfort to know I could go to a safe place. There would be many nights when I would take her up on her offer. Her listening ear and soothing words were calming.

I needed to tell Gary when he got home. We usually waited until Gary finished his late class at school to eat dinner. Generally, we recapped our day's happenings, but there was very little conversation at the table that night. Neither Scott nor I looked at each other and Gary was tired. I waited until we went to bed and knew that Scott would not hear us as I began to break the news. We lay together for a few moments. As I disclosed the conversation with Scott, I sobbed in Gary's arms as he held me.

Releasing me from his hug and looking at me quite surprised, he said, "What? How? Why? I don't get it. He's not a woman and he knows it."

"I don't know any more than you do. But it seems he's made up his mind," I sighed as I had no more tears.

"We need to trust God is still in control," he calmly told me. I could tell he was shaken by this as well as he continued to hug me tighter.

"What are we going to do? Where do we go from here?" I asked, hoping he would have some miraculous insight that hadn't been revealed before.

"I don't know," he said, sounding distant and questioning. That was a sleepless night. My mind kept going over the questions I had about this whole dilemma. I knew I had to know more. I would do my research, while Gary held the matter at arm's length. However, a couple of days later, I overheard a conversation he had with Scott. Gary was in his recliner, reading, when Scott approached him casually.

"Hey, Dad, where do you put the dinosaurs in the evolutionary scheme?"

Putting down his book, he looked up to answer him. "First of all, I don't believe they fit at all in the 'evolutionary scheme.' I do believe God created them and they were here coterminous with man."

Then, sounding more serious, Gary questioned him further. "Are you taking an evolutionary position? Don't you think God created everything?"

Reluctant to relax, Scott continued to stand in front of Gary as he answered.

"I do believe there is an evolutionary process. Things weren't always the way they are today. There's always change going on. Sometimes things didn't work out so there was change to accommodate."

Gary pursued the subject. "Do you believe there were mistakes?" Pausing, he continued. "Do you believe God created man and woman as they are?"

Scott was now uncomfortable with where the conversation was going. Folding his arms and shifting his weight, he answered. "No. We're always changing in some ways—nothing ever stays the same."

Gary took the opportunity to push further. "Do you think God made a mistake with you when he created you as a man? Would He make your body one way and your mind another way?"

Turning to walk away, he said, "Could happen."

I continued to seek fervently for help. We were now moving into a more desperate situation. My next source was a

Mom, I'm a Girl

Christian organization that helped homosexuals in dealing
with their problems. I had found their website on the Internet
and decided it was worth a try, at least. Perhaps they would
have some connections for transgender issues as well.

I went to a discussion group one night and afterward approached one of the counselors, again, a young man, who had
come out of homosexuality. In talking about the transgender
topic, I heard the same answer: "I'm not that familiar with it
but will talk with him." I was getting the picture that either
nobody knew about this or they didn't want to talk about it—
maybe both. This wasn't something that came up in many discussions, certainly not in Christian circles. When people would
ask about Scott in general conversation, I would answer in
vague terms. I was keeping Scott's "issue" close to the vest until
I could get a handle on the subject. Embarrassment entered the
picture, since I didn't know how people would react to Scott
and to us. What would they think of us as parents—especially
since we were in ministry? I kept praying for that neon sign or
loud voice from above that would direct me to that problem
solver who would take care of it all. Nothing. I was groping in
the dark.

Scott said less and less about his feelings unless I pushed
him, and then he'd speak only briefly. I mentioned the young
man at the center and Scott agreed, reluctantly, to talk with
him. After a few meetings he seemed to make a connection
with this fellow. Ah, maybe some light was breaking through?
But my moment of hope was dashed as I talked with the counselor after several more meetings.

"I'm not sure I'm doing much good for Scott," he told me as I handed him his check.

"Really?" I looked at him hopefully, thinking there might be something he missed.

"I thought he was making a connection with you," I went on. "He doesn't say much but what he does say is positive." *Oh, please, don't give up on him,* I thought. *I don't know where to go if you bail out!*

"Scott's made up his mind. We're talking in circles," he told me, shaking his head. I think he sensed the despair I was feeling at this moment. When Scott and I got in the car to go home we had another conversation.

"How do you feel things are going?" I was trying to sound more relaxed than I'm sure my face was showing.

"Hmm," he grumbled. "He's all right but he's not trans; he's a homo so he doesn't know anything about what I'm feeling." He ended the conversation and my hopes were dashed once again.

Scott was now well into his senior year and it was getting more and more evident that he was going into this full bore. His hair was longer, down past his shoulders, and he had made his flared pants into long skirts. However, since he mostly wore tight-fitting jeans, I was curious and puzzled. His explanation, "Because that's what all the girls wear."

Passing his room on my way to my bedroom one day I saw Scott sitting on his dresser, cross legged, typing on his computer. He looked relaxed, moving slightly to the music on his headphones. I stopped in my tracks, to process what I had just seen. Was he really sitting on his *dresser*? He often did random things like this. In fact, his favorite word was "random." Another act of "randomness" was to take his mattress off the bedframe and put it on the floor, removing the frame altogether. I set the pile of clothes I was carrying on the floor, backed up, and entered the room.

"Hey, Bug, what's going on?" I had found seizing the moments when not much was going on was the best time for talk. I still could not get my head around what he was doing.

"Oh, hey, Mom, not much—just talking with some friends. What's up?" he answered, taking off his earphones. He put them aside, indicating that he might be open for some conversation.

I approached with a smile. "Kind of an unusual place to sit."

"Yeah, I know but I can lean back against the wall and look out the window."

"OK, makes sense, I guess," I said leaning against the wall next to him. He was slightly higher than my eye level so I had to look up but it felt comfortable talking to him in this way.

"Mind if I ask you a question?" I asked inquisitively.

"Shoot."

"I'm just curious. Why do you want to be a girl? I mean, I can think of a few things I *don't* like about being a girl. So what's the draw for you?"

Tilting his head to the side and down, he answered thoughtfully, "Mostly it's because girls can express whatever they're feeling. They can cry when they want to or just not do anything. They can talk to their girlfriends and stuff. I dunno—they're just more emotional." From the wistfulness in his voice, I could tell he was struggling to put into words something he felt deeply.

"I get that. It's more acceptable for girls to be more emotional than guys. I guess that's something our society has put on us. But personally, I think it's OK for guys to express their emotions, too. In fact, I think it's cool," I said lightheartedly.

Patting him gently on the leg, I smiled and said, "Just think about it."

As I turned to leave the room, I heard him softly answer, sarcastically, "Sure, Mom." I left it there, realizing that was as close as I was going to get to an answer to my questions.

Well, he did think about it. Not long after that conversation, he came up with more surprises. I was in the kitchen preparing dinner. Scott came wandering in with a questioning look.

"How easy is it to get your name changed?" he asked very calmly.

"I suppose it's not that difficult, just costs money. Why? Are you thinking of changing your name?" I answered, again in my most disguised voice, masking my feeling of getting whacked with something I was totally unprepared for.

Then I asked rather casually, "What would you change it to?"

"Sydney Royal," he said with pride, looking at me with a big smile. "I like the name Sydney, like in Sydney, Australia and I like keeping the R so I'll just change that to Royal, like the lion," he said.

It would cost money to change his name, and money had been a big issue throughout these past months. We had told him we would provide everything he needed while living with us but that we would not support in any monetary fashion anything that condoned his behavior, including dresses and the like. He had garnered a good bit of support from his girlfriends who basically supplied him along those lines. When I reminded him of our agreement about what we would support, I thought it might deter him from changing his name for a while. But it did not. It took him a very short time to go through the simple process. After he completed the procedure he announced he would like us to address him by his new name.

My anger welled up. I was being pushed in too many directions. He was demanding we accept his appearance and support his decisions. *Good grief! What next?* I was beginning to realize he would be making more demands on us than we could comply with. *There are going to be other expectations. Where do we draw the line? Is there a line we can draw?*

After we all discussed the matter we agreed to *try* to abide by his request, but we said we couldn't guarantee anything since we had called him Scott for almost eighteen years. We concluded that since he had made a legal change, we would make the effort. We wouldn't, however, give in to his other request to change his addressed pronoun to "she." That was never going to change. The bombs kept coming as the "what next" happened.

"Mom, do you have any of those shoulder pads you used in your jackets?" he asked one day, nonchalantly.

"Sure, I've got several pairs. Do you need them for something?" I was immersed in a project for Sunday School so I wasn't giving full attention to the conversation. I couldn't imagine what he would want them for, maybe another sewing project?

"Oh, I'm just trying something out," he quipped.

I gave them to him and walked away as he headed to his bedroom. I didn't *want* to imagine, as my denial was in full bloom. By denying all of this I could maintain some semblance of sanity. My mind was engaged in a tug of war between loving him unconditionally and knowing I could not support his decision to make this change. Awhile later when I called him for dinner, he emerged from his bedroom. Gary and I both tried to hide the horror on our faces as he came out with breasts showing underneath his tank top, obviously made by my shoulder pads. Surprisingly, the thought that came into my mind was, *I always thought of doing that to enhance my A-cup, but he actually **did** it!*

Gary's reaction was more forthright than mine, as it usually is.

"Go back to your room and take those off!" he snapped. With his tone of voice and his look, I knew we were headed for something other than a peaceful meal. Scott complied this time but at breakfast he was wearing them again. He was off and running toward what he wanted and nothing was going to get in his way. He was definitely pushing the boundaries now and he knew it. As many more heated arguments followed, I tried to maintain some semblance of calm, but would cry out to God, ***What*** *is going on? This was not the way it was supposed to happen! Where are you? You were supposed to deliver all of us from this horrible situation!* ***Now*** *what?*

Feeling he had complied with our counseling efforts, Scott wanted to find one that met his criteria and that we pay for it. We agreed with reluctance. By this time we were grabbing at straws and thought maybe if he picked someone he connected with they could actually see through and help him on his terms. He found a transgender counselor on the Internet.

Since we were going to foot the bill, Gary and I felt we needed to meet the counselor and understand her position. Her office was part of her living quarters in a very old brick apartment building in downtown Portland, just across the river into Oregon. We turned the well-worn metal doorknob and pushed the odd-sounding buzzer on the intercom to announce our arrival. The old boards creaked underneath our feet as we walked up the steps in the musty-smelling old building. With each step, we became more anxious as to what we would find behind the door at the top of the second floor. She was prompt in answering her door after we knocked, gracious as she invited us in. Following her inside, we went through a beaded curtain into her living room. She had apparently been there for quite some time as her very small, cluttered apartment contained furniture left over from the '40s, maybe even the '30s. Her several floor-to-ceiling bookcases were packed with all sorts of books on sexuality, sexual behaviors, and psychology, titles like *Dealing With The Sexual Mind, Behaviors of the Sexual Male,* and *Psychology of Behavioral Activities of the Sexual Female.* Just by looking at the titles I realized how naive I was on this subject. But on the other hand, glad I was.

Her diminutive stature put me at ease. She looked more like a Rockwell grandmother than a sex therapist. Standing about five feet tall and about seventy-five years old, she was dressed in a print skirt with plain blouse, a cameo pin on the top buttonhole. A shawl draped over her shoulders. Her pleasant demeanor belied her forthrightness in getting down to business. She gestured with her hand to an overstuffed green couch, for us to sit down while she sat on her swivel desk chair. As she was speaking my eyes surveyed the room. *Yep, looks pretty much like a grandma's place.* There was just one other stuffed chair, green as well, an old-style, three-legged corner table with a lace doily under a stack of books. The only other table in the room held her computer with more books on the side. Not much room for anything else. I looked past her and could see her quite small kitchen, again through a heavily beaded curtain. The only other door had a full-length mirror and I guessed it led to her bedroom or the bathroom. I was going to ask to use the restroom to see which it was but decided against it. The floral-papered walls with brown molding on the top showed some water stains here and there, though most of the walls were covered with bookcases or her certificates. Sitting erect, she folded her hands in her lap. Our knees were practically touching hers as we sat across from her. Pushing her wire-rimmed glasses up her rather large nose, she looked at us, one at a time. Her quiet grandmotherly voice tried to put us at ease.

But we *weren't* at ease. Gary and I looked at each other. Our eyes meeting, we seemed to say to each other, *How did we end up here? What is she going to tell us?* Gary's eyebrows furrowed and I could feel my palms start to sweat. She must have sensed how uncomfortable we felt.

"I must tell you that very few who think they are transgender truly are." As she peered over her little glasses she continued. "I certainly will be able to discern this and would be willing to take on the case."

Her voice wasn't all that unpleasant and I felt myself being drawn to listen to her. She also continually flashed a little smile. All the time she was speaking, I was wondering, *Does this lady have a life outside of studying sex? Did she ever marry or have a family? Is she encouraging these people to do these things?* Before we left, she mentioned a form Scott could sign that would allow her to disclose information about their discussions if he agreed. Hence, the counseling began.

All during this time Scott exhibited a dichotomous nature. Around the house the bra thing was all he did that was truly feminine; he was never without his "breasts." Occasionally he would paint his nails and put on a little makeup now and then, but for the most part that was it. He talked in a normal voice and acted like he always had, stomping through the house. We would watch football games and he would get into it as usual, shouting at the TV. "Oh, geez, why did the ref call *that?!* Get your head out of your behind—it's football!" He would comment on the play selection and criticize the coaches so his conversations were like they had been all along. Of course, I couldn't say much against this because I make lots of comments during football games as well. There was nothing to indicate he was trying to acquire any real feminine behavior all the time.

One time Gary and I were in the garage, taking on a much-needed cleaning project. Gary's tool bench needed decluttering and I was organizing boxes when Scott barged through the garage door.

"I'm going on a date and he'll be here in just a few minutes. I'm your daughter and expect to be treated like it," he said. Swishing his hair back he looked at us with defiance.

Stunned at this latest development, we immediately stopped and looked at each other. A minute later his date showed up, parked his car at the curb, and walked up the driveway. Bringing him into the garage, Scott introduced us quickly as he walked by. But we noticed he talked in a different, softer tone. He acquired a certain air of being demure. What a change in attitude! I didn't know he could be so reserved. The walk was interesting as well. *I* don't have that much wiggle when I walk, but I guess he figured that was how it's done.

He only had a couple of these "dates," each time with a different boy. He would put on extra makeup but still wear jeans and tank tops to accentuate his breasts. Gary and I would be very polite as he made the introductions and tried to be as relaxed as possible.

After they left we would look at each other and shrug our shoulders. He never would tell us much about these fellows; where he met them, how old they were, or where they went to school. We never did much prodding as we saw them very little after the initial introduction. Occasionally, he bought a dress or skirt or other "girl-type" clothes but didn't wear them much, except for an infrequent date. We would treat him as we always had. When we went out in public, we were constantly aware that he wanted us to treat him as a girl and refer to him as "her" and "she." We studiously avoided that.

We were at a restaurant one afternoon having lunch. The conversation was light, small talk about what we had just done at the house. The waitress came over to get our order.

"Have we decided what looks good?" she asked as she took her pencil out.

Gary started to order. "Let's see. Mom, you wanted the soup and sandwich and . . . " he paused for a couple of seconds. During those few seconds both of our minds whirled with responses. *What do we say? She? He? Scott? Sydney?* Scott glared at Gary with a slight smirk on his face, quietly engaging him in a challenge.

"And what did you say you wanted?" Gary said, fidgeting with the menu as he looked across the table at Scott. Scott rattled off the order to the waitress and continued to look at Gary. Conversation shut down. But then he confronted us.

"Are you ashamed of me?" he asked, with disdain in his voice.

"We're just not sure how to handle all of this," said Gary. "We've had a son for eighteen years and now, all of a sudden, we're expected to act like we have a daughter."

After lunch as we left the restaurant, I thought, *Another otherwise nice occasion turned difficult, showing me to be inept in dealing with these situations.*

We were living with a situation that we knew was wrong and that it was not going to have a good ending if it continued on its present course.

Scott expected us to just make this switch with him and go along with everything because we as parents were supposed to be supportive of our children in difficult circumstances. In his mind this would be showing our love for him. Here was our biggest conflict: letting him know we loved him no matter what, on one hand, and on the other, letting him know that we could not go along with this decision he was making. In heated moments he would always come back at us, in a mocking tone, with the statement he had heard many times before and now applied to himself, "Love the sinner, hate the sin." In his mind, loving and supporting were one and the same, and because we didn't support him we didn't love him. Any actions contrary to what he wanted he would berate and mock. "Oh, that's right, this might be a *trans* thing." Our conversations became guarded.

What hurt the most was that I had lost the son I once had: the son I could joke with, play basketball with, go for a friendly walk with, and enjoy that special bond forged through the years. My heart yearned for those relaxing times when I didn't have to worry about what I did or said to him. My mother's heart was breaking because he wasn't happy; this was causing him pain and turmoil.

It became too much. Dropping to my knees over my bed, I broke down, sobbing. An image came to me. I saw myself as a little girl coming before the most compassionate Father on His chair, arms reaching out to me. I stretched out my arms holding a doll, representing my son, in my hands, and presented it to Him, tears streaming down my face, "Won't you please fix him? He's broken!"

His buddies had varied reactions, too. Some went along with the change; some didn't know how to handle it, visibly confused. A few took offense and cut off their friendship. Joel had been a great friend and took Scott's changes in stride. He was a laid-back kid and had learned to roll with some hard blows. His dad was a functioning alcoholic and his parents had gotten a divorce just a couple of years earlier. To him Scott's transition was something else he had to deal with. He and Scott were very close and I'm sure Joel wanted to do as much as he could to help Scott through this change.

One day Joel came to our house for the afternoon. "Hey, do you want to go over to my house and play video games?" Joel asked Scott. "I got this cool new game. Wait'll ya see it!" Since we didn't have all the video equipment Joel had, Scott was more than happy to oblige.

"Sure, let's go. Mom'll take us over to your house," Scott said as he started getting his coat on. Joel gathered up his things. Since I wanted to talk to Joel's mom, I had no problem driving them over.

We all entered Joel's house together. Scott was attired in his "feminine" manner. Michael was sitting on the couch playing a video game.

"Hey, Michael," Scott said with a smile as he looked down at him.

"Hi," Michael, Joel's younger brother, responded quietly. He turned his head just enough to acknowledge Scott but did not look at him directly. Immediately putting the remote down and getting up, he left the room saying as he left, "You can play if you want to." Michael was not supportive in any way, shape, or form of what Scott was doing.

It was interesting to note the dynamics of the group when Scott would get together with his friends. They seemed OK with his feminine demeanor and did refer to him as "she." They would joke around in the front yard, but if other friends from outside the neighborhood came by, it became very awkward; uncomfortable silence and downward looks.

It became clearer that they were all going their separate ways. Gradually, Scott became good friends with a couple of girls who took him under their wing. I looked at him from time to time with his "breasts," long hair, painted nails, and makeup and in one respect admired him. High school can be a very cruel environment. Kids can be outspoken and demeaning to anyone who is different, who doesn't fit their mold of what they think is cool. Scott did not fit into anyone's norm. He was definitely going against the grain. I'm sure he made many kids feel uncomfortable when he was around, what pronoun would they use? Should they assume he did girl things? Did he still like guy things? People like to fit people into little boxes and he certainly didn't fit into any of them.

I empathized to some extent because of my experiences in high school. But I had more kids who were like me than Scott did. I at least had teammates to hang out with whereas Scott had very few who extended their understanding and unconditional acceptance. In that way, I respected him for having the fortitude to do what he was doing under such difficult conditions.

In high school, peers are your world: how you fit in, how you're perceived by them, what groups accept you, and what groups don't. I know I wanted desperately to be accepted by the "in" crowd. I was different. I wasn't outgoing, pretty, and flirtatious with the boys. I made a few attempts to break into their circle with little success. It only made the contrast between us that much more apparent. As we all do, I sought out those more like me and began to accept myself for what I was.

Scott did the same; he found support at school, including an active LGBT group on campus in which he became very involved. This only spurred him to get as much counseling for his transition as possible.

After his first session with the new counselor, we were anxious to hear how things went. Scott was all smiles as he came through the door.

"How did it go? Do you like her?" I asked with trepidation.

"Yeah, she's really old but nice. She gave me a test and it said that I really am a girl," he remarked with satisfaction.

"Oh, really?" I wasn't sure if my heart just stopped or if it just came up in my throat. I couldn't say anything more.

Since it appeared he was going to get support from this counselor, I decided I had better start getting some for myself. Like any thinking person these days I headed for the Internet. I found a "chat room" (mind you this was way before Facebook) monitored by a woman who had dealt with a transgendered father. She started this website for people asking questions or passing on experiences that had helped them deal with problems related to this issue. I called and asked if there was someone she could recommend that I could talk to personally. She had a wonderful resource, Jim, who had come out of this situation. He was out-of-state but when I called he was most empathetic. He had written a book about his experiences as a transgender male and how God had led him through his recovery. After asking him many, many questions regarding Scott's position, I asked him to send the book, hoping Scott would read it and relate to it. He said he would be more than happy to and emphasized he would be available to talk anytime I felt the need. Could this possibly be the one connection God was sending to finally help Scott break free?

But another very dramatic event occurred that I hoped God would use to help him.

He had been seeing his counselor on a regular basis for about eight months or more. He wouldn't tell us much about the sessions, just bits and pieces. For example, he told us she was teaching him how talk with a more feminine tone and suggested he needed to dress more feminine. Apparently, they were getting along just fine until she laid the bombshell on him.

I had dropped him off as usual at her apartment and had returned a few minutes early, expecting to read for a few minutes before he came out to the car. The next thing I knew he was at the car and flaming mad.

"Get out of here! That woman is a b****!" he yelled as he got in the car and slammed the door. He crossed his arms across his chest and kept spouting obscenities. "I never want to see that woman again! She had the guts to tell me I'm not trans!" I figured I had best keep quiet and let the rampage take its course. That was one of the few times I had ever seen him that mad.

Later, Gary and I went down to talk with her. Sure enough, she had told him that. She felt he was more inclined to be "gender neutral," that is, not wanting to be labeled either male or female. She explained she saw no real passion toward being a woman, only wishing he could be. I asked about the test she supposedly gave him in the beginning. She looked at us questioningly and told us there is no such test but wished there was—it would make her job a lot easier. In the end it turned out picking a very experienced counselor actually worked against him. We hoped, again, that God was using this turn of events for His ultimate purpose.

Chapter 6

EXPECTATIONS

In his heart a man plans his course,
but the Lord determines his steps.
Proverbs 16:9

After this, I went back to the scriptures for comfort
and encouragement. Of course, I looked at the examples where
things turned out OK in the end because that's what I naturally
thought would occur in my case. God would give me the test
and things would turn out for the best—meaning, according to
my plan. I read about the disciples in the boat riding through
the storm. The storm came up, they were frightened, they cried
out to Jesus, and Jesus calmed the wild waves. Happy ending. Or Lazarus' death; he was in the grave, his sisters were in
pain and sadness, they cried out to Jesus, and He raised him
from the dead. Everybody rejoiced. I turned to the story of the
prodigal son who was arrogant and greedy, disrespecting his

father. He went away, ended up living in unhappiness, came back, the father took him in, and all was good again. Even the scripture verse, Romans 8:28, "For all things work together for good . . . " I took to mean that God would turn everything around for me and be good in the end. I saw God as the great "fixer," giving us a few tests to see if we would trust Him and then say, "OK, that's good, everything's all right now." My expectation was that He would change the *circumstances* around me. Though I did trust Him on a superficial level, I was giving mere assent to trust than to surrendering fully.

I remembered a story I once heard. A tightrope walker demonstrating his skills had just proved he could span a chasm before a crowd of people. He showed great prowess and strength as he walked steadily along the tiny wire. Everyone was amazed and gave their hearty approval by cheering and clapping. Upon returning, he turned to the crowd before him.

"You have just witnessed me walking across this crevasse. Would any of you like to trust me and climb on my back and walk to the other side?"

The crowd was stunned. "Oh, no," they all said, shaking their heads. "We're safe here."

Even though I had seen God in action through Bible stories, had been taught about His great deeds, and had read other people's stories about His deliverance, I still could not trust completely. The ground I was standing on was shaking and falling apart. I couldn't take that step and trust Him fully to get me across this mighty chasm I was facing.

I wrote in my journal, *"Chatting after prayer group, I made a couple of comments with friends about how we need to feel pain before we really change."* I had Scott in mind. Later, in that same entry, I said, *"Then I realized, too, He has to do the same thing to me. Can I count it all joy yet?"* I was still holding on desperately to *my plan* and having control, all the while trying to make additional plans as present plans started to unravel. I was clinging to the thought that God would turn Scott around and see us all through this storm with a happy ending. After all, doesn't God love us and want the best for us? Of course; the best would be to get us all back to "normal."

A lot of my hopes were based on all the expectations I had as we began our family. We had Scott when I was forty, figuring I had done all I wanted to do and was now ready to settle down. I had envisioned lots of things in our future, some of which did come to fruition: bike riding, skiing, and taking part in his school activities. As he began junior high I assumed the rest would come around as well; high school graduation and college, a career that used his many talents, girlfriends and eventual marriage. I had the future all laid out, according to my plans. I saw myself greeting grandchildren at the door, being the best grandparent ever, once I got through being a parent. I didn't want to think that there would be another plan. After all, my request was quite simple, to have a small, loving family and a nice ever-after. God would surely grant that, wouldn't He? Instead, I found out the old adage is true: "Life is what happens when you make other plans." I had a lot to learn about God's character and especially His love. I just didn't expect to learn it this way. My plans? Not so much.

Chapter 7

SENIOR YEAR

Surely there is a future,
and your hope will not be cut off.
Proverbs 23:18 (NASB)

Scott's senior year was tumultuous. He turned eighteen in September of that year. He could now be on his own. We had made it clear that at any time he felt he could no longer live under the current conditions, he was free to leave. However, until such time we expected him to fulfill certain duties around the house as a functioning member of the family. He was rebelling more and more against our authority, so he relished getting out. We discovered, however, he was already making choices that being eighteen allowed him to make. We had no idea how he got them but we discovered he was taking female hormones, prescribed by a doctor, and had been taking them for quite some time. I couldn't believe how manipulative he must have been to obtain them. How in the world was he getting these pills? What doctor would prescribe them? However he got them, they put his emotions in a tizzy. We had been noticing his change in behavior over the past months. He had become moody, easily annoyed, and quick-tempered. Little things, like misplacing his drawing pencils or friends not calling when expected, got him very upset, which only fueled more conflict. We had to be cautious with our words as they would easily set him off. One incident brought things to a head.

His sandy-blond hair was long by this time and he kept it straight, hanging naturally down to his shoulders. He wanted to dye it black and asked for my help. Since his hair had always been a bone of contention, Gary chose not to offer an opinion on the idea. I responded as a positive gesture, since he had asked for my help. We got out the box of color and read the directions. Entering the bathroom, I wondered what I was embarking upon, but I also thought it could be fun. It was a challenge to keep the black dye from splattering over everything, and we were not successful. We laughed as water sprayed all over the counter. Clothes were getting wet and the bathroom looked like a disaster area. Towels were strewn all over the counter. Scott's head was almost as big as the basin, so trying to keep the water only on his head was a real chore. In the midst of all this chaos, I felt so good laughing with him as we had so often done before.

"Put your head under the spigot. I can't get your hair wet enough," I giggled. He was already in a pretzeled position due to his five foot, ten-inch height. I pushed his head farther forward.

"Holy cow, Mom, I can't get any more bent over," he tried to say as water trickled in his mouth. "The water's getting in my eyes."

"Well, what do you expect? We have to get your whole head wet so your eyes will get wet."

"Hey, my hair's caught in the drain!" he gasped. We both burst into laughter. I struggled to keep reading the directions. Towels were getting stained, bottles, tubes, and instructions were thrown all over the bathroom. The pungent smell of dye permeated the air. Fortunately, I had prepared for the task by wearing old clothes. We finally got the job done and Scott came out to the living room where Gary was sitting. With a towel around his shoulders, hair wet and black, Scott stood in front of Gary as he sat in his swivel chair watching TV. Scott didn't say anything, just smiled slightly, waiting for a sign of approval. Gary looked up from the TV with little expression. Certainly, he gave no approval.

Scott began cursing at him. "Well, just f*** you!" he yelled.

Gary looked at him with quivering lips. "You don't talk to me like that! One more word like that and you're out of here!" Scott threw down his towel and cursed again with intensity, eyes fixed on Gary.

"That's it! You're out of here!" Gary bellowed as he leaned from his chair, glaring at Scott angrily, and pointed his finger toward the door.

"Fine!" Scott shouted as he stomped back to his room and slammed the door.

I panicked. My heart pounded in my chest. I couldn't believe what I had just witnessed between father and son. *Did Gary really mean it? Would Scott really leave? Where would he go?* I was petrified. I looked at Gary in his rage. He had not moved from his chair. His eyes were blazing mad as he kept his gaze on the floor. His face was red and his lips were still quivering.

I had to talk so I called Katie, my confidant.

"Oh, Katie! Gary just told Scott to leave! I don't know what to do!" I sobbed.

"What happened?"

"I don't know—it just happened. We were doing Scott's hair and things blew up. Gary and Scott got in a shouting match."

"Is Scott still there?"

"Yes, he's still here. I don't know where he would go," I said, my voice still shaking.

"Just keep an eye on him tonight and see what happens in the morning. We'll be praying for you," she said softly as we ended the conversation.

Though sleep didn't come, morning did come and Scott was still in his room. The three of us had a chance to talk things out. He asked about any legal obligations we had to care for him beyond his eighteenth birthday. We pointed out he was considered an adult. He could make his own choice since we were under no mandate, even if he was still in school. It seemed at that moment that being eighteen and able to be on your own might not be all that great. He mentioned a few options but none were realistic. At the end of the discussion, we agreed he would complete the school year at home and leave after graduation. At least that would give him some time to try to arrange a place. Gary and I knew we were in for a rough several months.

During those months I cried a lot, feeling God distant. Why wasn't He answering my prayers? Why wasn't there any help coming? Things were escalating, rather than getting better as I had anticipated. Scott was a victim of tangled emotions and we got the backlash. He compelled us more and more frequently to conform to his mode of thinking. His argument was always, "I'm your daughter; don't you love me? Aren't you going to protect me?"

On one occasion, he planned to try out for the girls' tennis team. *This will be interesting*, I thought. *You're really going to try out for a **girls'** team?* When a physical was required, I wondered, *What's the doctor going to put on your exam report? And how is the coach going to handle this?* But I said I would take him for an exam. Since we didn't have a regular doctor we went to the urgent care center to get it taken care of quickly. Walking into the office, I was apprehensive how the visit would go. I wondered if I should say anything or just let things ride. I decided to ask Scott about some of my concerns.

"I thought the rules stated that only girls could participate on a girls' team. Does the coach know about this?"

"Yeah, and she said she would let me try out, accepting me as any other girl," he told me defiantly. He looked me squarely in my eyes, as if to say, *She does, even if you don't.*

"What would you do if you played and the other coach found out and protested?" I tried again, wanting him to realize he was putting other people at risk for his own pleasure.

"That's their problem," he answered flatly. He went back to reading his magazine.

I never saw the report nor did I query Scott as to what the doctor put down. He did become the manager of the girls' team.

Chapter 8

CHRISTMAS HEARTBREAK

My soul weeps because of grief; strengthen
me according to Thy word.
Psalm 119:28 (NASB)

The Christmas holidays have always been a joyous occasion in my life. Our family followed many Swedish traditions, including the smorgasbord. There were brown beans, herring, Swedish meatballs, and lutefisk, later dropped due to the popular demand of the younger generation. Music was an essential part of our celebration since my aunts and uncles were wonderful musicians on violin, piano, and accordion. As the melodies started, the adults danced to polka and schottische tunes while the kids pretended to. Then there was the Lucia bride, a Swedish tradition involving a young maiden. Turning the lights down low, we began to sing the traditional song. In dramatic fashion, the youngest girl in the family would make her appearance, playing the part of the Lucia bride. She was dressed in a simple white gown with a red sash, a glowing crown of candles on her head.

"Isn't she cute?" one aunt would remark to another.

"The white gown fits her perfectly."

"The next youngest will be the bride next year. Do you know who that will be?"

"She's doing very well, balancing the cookies on that tray."

As we all sat around in a circle, she served the family spritz cookies as we sang "Santa Lucia." These were memories I have treasured as far back as I can remember, and I had always wished that one day my children would experience and cherish those treasured traditions, too.

Scott was the youngest of the next generation to come along. We lived out of state until he was five so he didn't see his cousins or second cousins very often. When we did come up for the holidays, he found it a strain to make their acquaintance again. The other kids considered him a stranger. However, he made the effort to be friendly and eventually the ice was broken. At that age, the traditions didn't matter to him. All that mattered was that Santa Claus showed up with his present. That made everything right.

When we moved into the area, he did experience some camaraderie with one or two of his cousins but never a close bond as I had with my cousins. As he grew older, he was never excited about the family gatherings.

He attended the family celebration his junior year, but during his senior year Christmas left me tied up in knots. My refuge was the family gathering, the last place Scott wanted to be.

He had announced well in advance that he was not going; he was going to Seattle to visit Johnny.

Scott had met Johnny at a Furry gathering some time ago. We had not met "him" but Scott filled us in. Johnny was transitioning, female to male. They texted constantly and I often heard conversations on the phone well into the night. To say they had grown close is to put it mildly. They had much in common, no doubt, but the one big difference was their home situation. Johnny had acceptance from most of her family whereas Scott did not. That only added fuel to Scott's burning embers of resentment. I could understand why he would rather be with Johnny than us.

Through a later conversation, I discovered something interesting. He said he didn't like other "trans" people; they were "over the top." They tried too hard; their "outlandish" appearance really turned him off. He said it even surprised him that he enjoyed being with Johnny.

It was fine with us to make the trip, but then he asked for money to get there. We knew he had money. We had found several hundred dollars neatly rolled up in his dresser not long before all this transpired. He refused to spend any of it, however, as he was saving every penny for his transition. We reminded him that our agreement was to provide for him while he was still living with us but anything extra was his responsibility. That included entertainment, feminine clothes, makeup, anything outside the realm of essentials.

Scott let it go for the moment. Later, he mentioned he wanted a warmer jacket for his trip. Since he didn't have a heavy jacket, and it was quite a cold winter, I agreed to go shopping with him. My one stipulation was that we buy a man's jacket. He agreed.

We started in the men's department. After wandering around with him, not seriously looking at anything, I knew I had been duped.

"What about this one?" I asked, holding up a plain, black, hooded jacket. He shrugged it off, sauntering away. I realized I had fallen into wishful thinking in taking on this task. As we drifted into the women's department I again mentioned our agreement. He wasn't listening.

"Hey, Mom! Look at this one—really cool!" he exclaimed as he picked one off the rack. "It's really rad!" He held it next to him to size it up.

"That's not what I had in mind," I said sternly as I scanned the pink, knee-length, furry, quilted, buttoned jacket. Hands on my hips, I felt my brows beginning to furrow as I turned away.

"Yeah, I'm just sure," he said as he hung the jacket back on the rack. "Too feminine, huh?" he stated sarcastically.

"We agreed that those clothes would be out of your pocket. We'll look at some others," I told him as I continued to walk over to more neutral styles.

"What about this one? Masculine enough? Meet your approval?" he quizzed as he held up a zippered, black, hip-length, down jacket. It was considerably less feminine.

"Yes, that's great," I agreed, relieved that we had found something we could compromise on, once again ending a frustrating and anxious situation. That coat served him well over the next weeks, especially that Christmas holiday.

He made arrangements to stay with Johnny several days. However, he had no transportation. He asked us for money again and we reiterated the ground rules. It was up to him to get up there. It was more and more evident that he would blame us for any hardship he was going through and make us the bad guys in every circumstance.

"You're not using all the cars, just let me take your car, Mom. Heck, I'm not going to be gone that long and you go up there all the time—it's no big deal," he pleaded his case.

"We've already told you we are not letting you take the car. There are other ways—take the bus, take the train." I heard my voice getting louder as my hands waved madly in gestures. It was hard disguising my frustration, especially knowing he had the resources to do this.

"Fine! I'll hitchhike! Can you at least give me a piece of cardboard and a pen?! I'm sure *someone* will take pity on me," he shot back, scowling as he turned on his heels and stormed out of the room. I was in the other room when I saw him pass by toward the front door with his backpack and sign. He had a look of defiance as he came to the door and pulled his knitted cap over his ears. He didn't say anything as he slammed the door behind him. I was torn again with conflicting emotions; *I can't back down now—I've got to stick with my word. Please don't do this. Think about what could happen!* Following him to the door, I opened it only to see him walk dejectedly down the street. The emotions of his rejection and my mother's love clashed. I cried out again, *Oh, God, what have I done? Where is he going? Please take care of him!* Gary came over and hugged me and said quietly, "Let him go."

I hoped we would hear something while he was gone. But nothing; no phone call, no email—silence. I wasn't even sure when he was coming home. The next week I thought about him constantly. Then the phone rang. He called to ask us to pick him up at the train station. He told us then that some of Johnny's relatives had been coming through the night he left and had picked him up. We were relieved that he had been safe on that journey. As I entered the train depot parking lot I spotted him on a bench outside the station. His head was down, his backpack next to him. He was clutching a stuffed animal. Spotting me, he walked over to the car just as I pulled to a stop, silently opened the door, and got in. The ride home was quiet.

"So, how was it?" I asked, just to break the ice. I knew I was opening myself up for further antagonism.

"A lot better than it is down here," he said softly, looking away from me out the window. "He's got a cool family. His dad's pretty laid back. They even gave me some presents."

"Well, glad to have you home. We missed you," I said. I looked at my son longingly, wanting to see that smile of affection and warm gaze that I had known. I remembered when he was younger how he would greet me after being separated for a while. His eyes would light up, his smile was ear to ear, and then he would wrap me in a big hug. But this time there was no smile and no hug.

"Yeah, I'm sure," he said with no emotion, glancing sideways at me. He turned back toward the window and what I saw was his knitted hat with the cat ears, his long hair straggling from beneath. I'm not sure whether it was colder outside or inside the car as we finished the drive home.

As we drove in silence, memories ran through my mind; the dancing, the laughter, the hugs, the joy of being with family. How I ached to have him enjoy the holidays with us as I had envisioned. But like so many things lately, life was taking a much different course than I had ever imagined. My heart yearned for the warmth and happiness of past years but instead I felt the icy chill and despair of reality.

New Year's Day came and after the holidays routine returned. Several weeks later, Gary and I were at the gym. We had left Scott in his room, where he had been spending a great deal of time the past several days. We came home to a shocking discovery.

Gary had put a small whiteboard in the dining room that we often used for reminders or notes to let each other know our whereabouts. This night it contained a message that sent us both into a panic. "So sorry, mom and dad—at the hospital," next to a picture of his Furry character with tears. We didn't know what to think. What could possibly have happened? There was nothing out of place, as far as we could tell. Nothing to indicate an accident or incident of any kind. What could it be? Where was he? We quickly called the hospitals in town and found out where he was. We raced up to see him. My heart and my head were pounding; *What would he look like? What would I say to him? Would he even want to see us?* Neither of us said anything as we drove the short distance to the hospital.

We learned the rest of the story from one of the hospital attendants. Scott had been on the phone with one of his close girlfriends and had apparently mentioned death or dying, and sounded depressed. She casually asked for his address, since she was from out of town. After they hung up she called 9-1-1 and told them the situation and the address. An ambulance took him to the hospital. At least he had thought enough to let us know where he was. But I had no idea what to say, how to talk with him; I was unprepared for any of this.

The room they put him in was stark and surreal. It was totally bare, the size of a very small bedroom. The naked walls were a light shade of green. The bed consisted of a mattress on a wooden box frame with one sheet. There were no chairs, so we brought a couple in. We looked at each other—he on the bed, Gary and I on the chairs.

Casually sitting on the bed, legs crossed, and arms folded, with no expression he started the conversation.

"They have to keep me for forty-eight hours, for observation; that's the procedure for attempted suicide. It really wasn't, so whoever called had it wrong," he explained. He didn't seem upset and didn't know exactly how it had all come about.

"Can we get you anything?" I felt so dumb asking any questions. *This was not like visiting a sick person or someone who just had an accident.*

"Are you feeling OK?" *Of course, he's not feeling OK,* I thought. *Of course, there's nothing we can get. He's depressed, he's angry at us, and probably doesn't even want to see us.*

"Mom, I'm sitting in a bare room, on a bed in hospital garb because they think I'm going to kill myself. What do *you* think?" He just sat there, head down, elbows on his knees. A picture of dejection. He barely looked at us when he spoke. His "garb" was the typical scrubs, light green top and bottom, and socks. My heart did flip flops. I wanted so badly to hold him and tell him everything would be OK. But that was impossible—he didn't want me to hold him and I could not even convince *myself* things would be OK. I kept looking at him but his eyes avoided me. The walls became more bleak as I stared at them. Lots of silence and heavy breathing. I kept wondering about all the possible outcomes of this situation, none being good.

Gary finally got up to see if he could get any more information. So late at night, people who knew what was going on were few and far between. He spoke with another attendant who told us they were looking for an available space in the mental ward. After further checking, we were informed there were no beds available in Vancouver; he was going to be transferred to Tacoma, the closest facility with availability.

"What do you mean, Tacoma? For how long?" we asked, with obvious confusion. Tacoma was two hours away.

"They'll keep him here tonight and then transport him tomorrow. I can't say for sure but more than likely they'll want to keep him for a week, maybe more, for observation." He sensed our concern, frustration, and confusion but wasn't able to give much comfort. He knew we wanted more answers but he was just the attendant, not qualified to go into any details. With nothing more we could do, we stayed a short time longer, then left. On the way home there were only questions between us and no answers. The only positive thing we could come up with was that possibly a professional person, doctor, psychiatrist, counselor, might see through this and give him some counseling. That was the hope we clung to.

We waited through two weeks of silence. Then came the call. It was the call we were waiting for, but certainly not the call we expected. Gary answered the cell phone, since I was driving.

"Yes, we can come get him," he said. Then he asked with expectancy, "Did you find any reason for his behavior or have you made any diagnosis?"

I almost ran off the road with his next outburst.

"Are you kidding me?! You're the one who's mixed up! Yes, we'll be there."

"What did he say?" I asked, trying to keep driving while my mind was anywhere but on the road.

"He said he's doing fine—he's OK. *We're* the problem!" He went on to restate what the doctor had told him but he had a hard time remaining civil. According to the doctors, our opposition to Scott's transition was the source of the problem. As Gary continued to express his anger, I could only feel more despair. My mother's heart was breaking for my child who so desperately needed help. We couldn't find anybody to come alongside and offer that help.

Another long drive. Gary uttered more irritation at the "professionals." It was more frustration and disappointment than anger as we had both been hopeful we could get some help with this whole issue. Gary was expressing his anger verbally, but I held my doubts and fears inside. *What now? How do we handle this when he gets home? What will he be like? Will he feel validated for what he's doing and continue to blame us?* On the way home with Scott, we had more disappointment and the confirmation of fear.

Finally breaking the ice, Scott leaned forward from his backseat position. I had been noticing his expression was rather upbeat, as opposed to the depression I somewhat expected.

"Yeah, they treated me great. Had my own room, had a recreation hall—hung out with the girls; food was good, too. They made me feel really good. Oh, sure—had to go through their ritual counseling but that was OK. Had better treatment there than at home," he related. He made it sound as if he had had a two-week vacation and now was coming back to reality. *Is there no help anywhere? If there isn't any professional help, where do we go? Who do we try next?* We were clearly out of options.

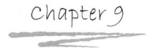

SCHOOL ISSUES

But the Lord stood at my side and gave me strength.
2 Timothy 4:17a

Options? I continued to chat with the people on the Internet forum, searching for any piece of new information or insight. Still, my prayers seemed to go unheeded as things continued to get worse. I knew God's hand was in this. How He was going to work this all out, I had no clue. I was always reaching for His hand but couldn't feel His touch.

Scott returned to school, for the most part. Apparently, he was missing quite a bit. I would get messages on the phone letting me know my "child was not in attendance" that day. I quizzed him on these occasions.

"I got a call from school today saying you weren't there. What's up?"

"Oh, those freakin' people get all upset if you're not there first period when they take attendance for the whole day. So I was a little late and came to second period. It's no big deal," he said.

Well, it turned out to be not so trivial. The next call was from the principal requesting a conference with us. As Scott and I entered the school building, I had more apprehension than Scott did, perhaps because he anticipated the purpose of the meeting. Greeting us warmly at the door of his office, the principal directed us to some comfortable chairs opposite his big oak desk. He then walked behind it and sat down in his overstuffed office chair. From his grim demeanor I knew this was not going to go well. As I sat down I could feel myself getting sweaty under the arms. I hoped my deodorant was working. He was pleasant enough as he made an effort for small talk. I tried to look relaxed in the leather chair but found myself leaning forward, sitting on the edge. He took a moment before he got to the matter. Leaning over his desk, hands folded in front of him, he began.

"The reason for my concern," he started, addressing Scott, "is that you are in danger of not graduating due to lack of attendance and failing grades." He was looking very businesslike at Scott. Pulling out some papers, he continued, his voice calm and patient.

"Your attendance has been very erratic lately, amounting to a month lost in class time. You are failing two classes and in danger of failing another," he pointed out.

Thoughts raced through my head, *What? You have got to be kidding me! Where was he if he hasn't been in school? He's been a good student—where's this coming from?* I tried to keep a straight face and not let my jaw drop, but my expression changed when I turned to look at Scott. He was slouched in his chair with a scowl on his face, his face turned squarely to the principal. He obviously knew the information was correct as there was no effort to countermand what had been said.

"Scott, is this true?" My voice matched my look of questioning.

"Yeah, I guess, if he says so." Scott turned to answer as if it were no big deal. No change in expression, no raised voice, just a "so what" attitude.

After a long silence, the principal probably saw he wasn't going to get much conversation out of Scott. He proposed some options.

"There are a couple of things you can do. You can get a certificate of completion, which means you completed high school but did not get a diploma or graduate. Or you can pick up credits on your missing classes online and complete your senior project. I can get you the specifics on that if that's what you want. It would take extra work but it would be doable." I appreciated the fact that he was willing to salvage what he could for Scott to get him to graduate.

"Think about it and let me know what you want to do," he said as he stood up, signaling the end of our visit. Looking at me he said, "Do you have any questions, Mrs. Glenney?"

"No, not at this point. Thanks so much for your help," I answered as we shook hands and turned toward the door. *Questions? Yeah, a lot of them but none that I think you can answer.*

He did enroll in the online class and did talk to his teachers about his classes, so things seemed to settle down, as far as I knew. Gary and I talked with him more about his school work in order to keep on top of things. Graduation was our top priority. Scott had another priority.

He had mentioned going to the prom but I tried not to put much stock in it. I hadn't received any more calls regarding his attendance so I started to relax—until another call from the principal. He wanted to see us again. *Good grief! What now?* I thought as my heart skipped a beat. My mind scrambled in all directions. As far as I knew he was on track for everything academically. Again, Scott and I went to meet with him. Things looked all too familiar. There was the friendly secretary, the cordial greeting from the principal, and the same overstuffed chair behind a big, oval, oak desk. We took the same seats as he took his place. Leaning back in his chair, he fidgeted with a pencil in his hands. I glanced over at Scott. He sat expressionless, dressed in his cat-ears knit hat, tank top, sweat jacket, and jeans. His arms were folded across his chest.

"The prom is coming up and I understand you're planning on going," said the principal. "Is that correct?" He looked at Scott questioningly.

"Yes," Scott answered with little emotion. Scott had made it crystal clear from the beginning that there was no love lost in his relationship with this man. I expected few words.

"I don't have a problem with that; you're certainly free to attend," he responded. "My concern is with the other students. I want to make sure that they feel comfortable and can enjoy this event as much as possible." Leaning back in his chair, he was trying to make this a pleasant conversation, choosing his words carefully. His voice was calming as he continued. "My only worry is with the lavatory facilities. We do have gender-designated restrooms. I think you can understand the circumstances here."

Scott sat back in his chair, put his hand behind his neck, and cocked his head aside. As I glanced over it seemed he was just daring the principal to go further into the explanation although he knew where he was headed. The principal kept his cool.

"Even though your appearance is female, I'm not sure all the female students would feel comfortable with you using the facilities. So to stave off any situations that might occur, we would ask that you use the non-gendered restroom, which is just down the hall. Would that be a problem for you?" He gave a forced smile.

"No," Scott replied, as he only looked at the principal.

"I just wanted to make sure that this is an event everyone can enjoy." He stood up, smiling, extending his hand signaling the end of the visit.

"Thanks so much for coming in."

Heading toward the car, several thoughts came to mind. *What if we hadn't had this conversation and he **did** use the girl's restroom? Would there have been repercussions from the girls and possibly parents? Which restroom does he use in other places?*

"So, what do you think about that?" I asked, trying to sound nonchalant.

"Yeah, Mom, like you *haven't* thought about this before? You don't know how hard it is trying to find a bathroom I can

use without *disturbing* somebody. Yeah, I know all about it."
He sounded put off and annoyed that I'd broached the subject. He was right. I had no idea what he was experiencing
and could only imagine what kind of looks he got from other
kids and the awkward situations he placed himself in. This was
much different from the life I had envisioned for my son going
through high school.

The day of the prom was fast approaching. Scott was getting more and more excited and I was getting more and more
uneasy. Most of the anxiety was in the anticipation of seeing
him outfitted so completely as a girl. The more he talked about
it the more thrilled he was with the idea. He couldn't decide
what kind of dress he should get, if he should wear his hair up
or down, or what color he should paint his nails. I was most
curious about his date. My fleeting thought was, *Would there
be a boy in this picture?* He settled that question as he said he
was going with one of his girlfriends. He had several close girlfriends, but the one he mentioned wasn't one of them.

I was not familiar with this girl, though I had met most of
those girls he was hanging around with. They were all helping
him through this "joyous" experience, and he was spending
more time with them after school. He would come home with
various items, such as purses, makeup, or a simple change in
hairstyle. Scott took Shelly (his "BFF") on a shopping trip for
the dress. It was a major highlight. Feeling quite accomplished
with a thrift store purchase, along with shoes and some acces-
sories, he was anxious to show me.

"Hey, Mom!" I heard him yell, slamming the door behind
him.

"Yes, I'm right here. What's up?" I looked up from reading the newspaper. I had been taking a few relaxing minutes in the living room and had just settled in to enjoy a little break. I didn't want to sound imposed upon so I tried to put anticipation in my voice. But I really don't think he would have noticed one way or the other as he chattered right on.

"Look at this dress! Neat, huh? It'll look really cool with these shoes. And I only paid ten dollars for the whole thing!"

I wasn't sure if he was more impressed with the fact he spent so little or with the dress selection. He took the dress out and showed it to me, expecting my affirmation of his shopping prowess. I just smiled as he revealed the modest, black dress.

Here we go again, I thought. *Once again, I'm put in a spot where I need to agree with his choice of feminine clothing. Do I really want to go there? Do I really want to make a big deal about this? He's all excited and I'm supposed to be, too. He's going to do this, so I guess I can be somewhat positive.*

"Yeah, this is nice. Wow, only ten dollars. Done good, kid."

"Thanks—I thought so, too."

My answer was good enough as he continued to beam, putting the dress back in the sack and going back happily into his bedroom. The newspaper slumped into my lap. Laying my head back on the couch, I closed my eyes, and sighed. *Lord, what am I doing? I don't want to push him away any more than I have but I can't affirm what he's doing. Just give me **something** to go on.*

The long-awaited day finally arrived. He spent a long time doing his nails—a glowing red. Then he hollered from the bathroom.

"Can you help me here, Mom?" peering into the mirror. "I want this to really look nice but I can't get it right," he said, fiddling with his mascara. "How are you supposed to get this on without getting it into your eyes?"

"You're asking *me*? I don't know much more than *you* do about this stuff."

"Well, you're a woman—you should know."

"Just because I'm a woman doesn't mean I know about makeup. Have you seen how much makeup I wear? I don't get enough practice to be much better at it than you."

I peered over his shoulder, trying not to snicker at his facial contortions. I realized I probably look the same way trying to get that sticky junk on what few eyelashes I have. I left the room, not wanting to be of any more help.

As I sat in the living room reading the sports section, trying to distract myself, my mind began to wander. My thoughts turned to my dreams of this day. They certainly hadn't looked like this. I didn't go to my prom, so I had looked forward to my son enjoying this wonderful night with a special "someone." He would look so handsome in his rented tux. I would make sure his tie was straight, his cummerbund fit just so, and his boutonniere was in the right spot. Renting his tux would be one of many details he would have taken care of. Trying to figure out what kind of corsage would go with her dress would be a major dilemma. There would be money for food and little gifts to make this night extra special for her. However, he would have been saving for this occasion for quite a while so it would be money gladly spent.

Back to reality.

Coming down the hallway, he was all smiles. Looking up from grading his papers and peering over his glasses, Gary glanced at Scott and went back to his papers. I gazed at Scott. I thought he had done a good job with the makeup. He had previously gone through electrolysis, so his facial hair wasn't an issue. The foundation was blended in to hide what little residue of hair there was. His lipstick wasn't outlandish, just enough red to make it noticeable. The mascara was a little heavy but not bad. His shoulder-length, sandy blond hair was much as he normally wore it: parted on one side and tucked behind his ears with a little more curl on the ends than usual. The dress was very simple—sleeveless, black, simply rounded at the neck with silver shimmers on the bodice, the loose-fitting skirt draping lightly to his knees. Black sandals finished the outfit. Not exactly what I had envisioned my son wearing on his prom night. His date arrived and rang the doorbell. He was at the door in a nanosecond. Opening the door, he rushed out, without even inviting the girl in.

"I'll see you guys later! Don't wait up—don't know when I'll be back!" he called back.

As the door slammed, I realized it slammed shut on another dream.

Scott on his prom night

Chapter 10

GRADUATION

For I know the plans I have for you,"
declares the Lord,
"plans to prosper you and not to harm you,
plans to give you hope and a future.
Jeremiah 29:11

Graduation is a time for rejoicing, celebrating achievements for time spent in arduous work over twelve years. For parents, it is a time for reflection and anticipation of the next chapter of our children's lives. My reflections were tainted by what had transpired during the past several years, my vision clouded by tears of what was to come in my child's tumultuous life.

It was a cool day with intermittent showers. The graduation ceremony took place in the football stadium. We arrived early enough to see him before he got seated with the rest of his class. He asked me to take a few pictures. Gary, meanwhile, strolled over to the covered seating area to save us seats. Before I turned my attention to Scott I glanced back at Gary and I noticed his demeanor was rather downcast. I could see he was struggling with this whole event. Settling down in the white plastic chair under the tent, he adjusted his hat. He pulled his coat around him to keep the chill off. Folding his hands in his lap he bent forward and kept his eyes on the ground.

I was snapped back to the moment with Scott's shouts, "Mom, take a picture of the caps—they are so cool!" he yelled. "Look at all the stuff these guys put on 'em! Just put the camera over your head to get the tops," he shouted, maneuvering around the crowd. His Mountain View High graduation cap was quite ornately designed, complete with lots of Pookeys. One Pookey was jumping for joy with arms and legs in the air, another was standing very arrogantly with hands on his hips, and a bigger one with head only, showed a huge grin. All these pictures were set against a backdrop of mountain scenery, textbooks, and notebooks, so very creative on the small mortarboard.

"Which photos do you want?" I asked, trying to stay on my feet as the raucous students were knocking me around.

"Take as many as you can!" he yelled over the crowd. "Hey—get us in this shot," he said, leaning his head against the shoulder of a girlfriend.

He was obviously having a good time, for which I was glad, but I had other feelings. I was grateful he was able to graduate. However, it still took me aback seeing him dressed in the white cap and gown worn by all the girls. Handing the camera to Scott, to signal the end of my picture-taking task, I made my way back to Gary. Looking up and giving me a half smile, he pulled my chair closer to him. I smiled back and patted his knee as I took my seat. Neither of us said anything as we anticipated the graduates crossing the stage to receive their diplomas. When they called out "Sydney Glenney," I had to think a minute. Who was that? Good question. Did *he* even know?

My journal entries:

Sunday, June 10

It is finally here—the day I have looked forward to for many years, but, oh how much different this is than what I had envisioned. But then it's not always about dreams, it's about reality. Last Sunday, he went to baccalaureate (which surprised us). It was, I'm sure, the hand of God. Everything that was said could pierce right through him if he was listening. We were both praying the whole time, "God, use these words; store them up in his heart and soul—"Your word will not return void." It certainly tore into us as we saw him in his white gown.

Friday, June 15

Graduation has now come and gone and I've tried not to dwell on it. It is what it has come to be—another event to be filed away under "what could have been." So I close my eyes, close the file drawer, and go on to today. It's getting to be a pretty full file and I'm sure will be a lot bigger before everything is done. But that file is brought before the Lord and forgotten "as to those things that are behind." Scott said he was picking out a picture for the slide show for graduation and I wanted to see it (the show) but I didn't. But he did show a few of them to me. Going through those pictures of younger years, it seemed his memories of those events were jaded. He's telling me a different version of what I remember happening. I'm doubting now even the relationship I thought we had. I thought the things we did as a family, he enjoyed. But did he really? I can't go through the albums now without looking at them differently—it's like the memories, as the pictures, have yellowed and taken on a different tone. Good memories? Hard to find—yet another wound that seems to heal but festers from time to time.

The thought looming in front of me was following through with our decision made earlier regarding him leaving. That scared me. He had mentioned staying with friends. But in reality I knew he had made no plans and had no idea where he was going. We didn't have much discussion. He seemed OK with just heading down to Portland. He had said many times how he liked Portland much better than Vancouver and would like to live there.

Scott's driver's license showing his name and gender changes

Only a few weeks after graduation the day came for his departure. The day was a typical June day—warm, sunny, with a slight breeze, and few clouds in the sky. Great day for a bike ride, I thought. Scott *was* taking a bike ride, but not for pleasure.

"What all are you taking?" I asked, watching him put things into his backpack. Opening up his bureau drawer, he selected his usual tank tops, a couple of sweatshirts, and jeans. "You don't need to take *everything*. You know you can come back and get things."

"I know, Mom—just the essentials—a few changes of clothes and stuff." He continued to rummage through his drawer, picking at random a few more light pieces of clothing that would fit in his medium-sized, brown canvas bag. He had used that bag mostly for books but now it was his suitcase.

"I'm not taking my computer 'cause I don't think I'll be any place secure," he said, stuffing things in the bag. "I'll come get it when I know where I'll be."

"That's fine—come back anytime for it," I said. After a slight pause I added, "You know I'll be thinking about you," trying not to sound too "motherly."

"Mom, I'll be fine," he answered with no concern. "It's not like I'm leaving the state, or anything." *Thank goodness,* I thought.

I walked him to the front door.

"You know we love you and you're welcome anytime," Gary told him sincerely.

"I know, Dad, love you, too," was his response as he headed out to get his bike. Hopping on, he was on his way. I was hoping he would look back for one more look but he didn't.

As he rode down the driveway and down the street, I wanted to bawl. My heart was aching, my head pounding with dire thoughts. *Where will he go? What will he do? Will he be safe? He's still my baby! What will he eat? Will he be taken in by the wrong crowd? I don't want him to go! Come back soon, Bug.*

Gary and I went back into the house to resume our routine. But before we did, we looked at each other, as if to say "Did we do the right thing?" and then hugged for the longest time. Tears finally came.

Some thoughts from the journal:

Truly a new phase has begun and it really hasn't hit yet. Gary is still wrestling with the past and I keep telling him not to go there. I hope he listens. I'm sure I'll have a meltdown before too long—just part of the process. Be faithful and leave the results to God. Oh, Lord, keep me faithful.

Chapter 11

EMAILS AND DINAH

A gentle answer turns away wrath.
Proverbs 15:1a

After Scott had moved out of the house I would look forward to any communication with him. One day, doing the dishes, my eyes wandered to the computer in the back room, just beyond the kitchen. Scott had been keeping me "tuned in" via emails and I wondered if he had sent anything recently. He was quite open to sharing his thoughts, although I'm sure it was only a glimpse of what was going on in his head. I missed so much the deep conversations we used to have, especially sitting in the car in the driveway.

We would start talking about something on the way home and as we approached the house, we would just be getting to the heart of the matter, so we stayed in the car, not wanting to disrupt our train of thought. Sometimes it would last an hour or more. On one occasion, Gary stuck his head out the front door, reminding me of my high school days when my boyfriend and I would be in the car in my parents' driveway "just talking" and my dad would stick his head out the door. If I didn't come in right away Dad would blink the porch light letting me know "that's quite enough" and I had better come inside. Gary never did blink the light, though. As we started one of these conversations, Scott was in his first year of high school. I had just pulled into the driveway and turned off the car when he began.

"I know you're going to quote the Bible on this but what's so bad about homosexuals?" he questioned.

"You mean, other than God said it was wrong?" I answered shifting my body to look at him directly.

"Doesn't that come from the Old Testament and are we still living by those laws? If we are, shouldn't we be stoning people and putting kids to death because they were bad and all sorts of things?" he retorted.

"No, we're not living under those laws, but homosexuality is mentioned in the New Testament as well and it's mentioned with other sins," I explained.

"Yeah, well, for people who don't believe the Bible it's OK. So there's really no other reason that it's bad or wrong except for Christianity and the Bible," he argued.

This conversation continued for quite some time as we talked back and forth about the morality of the issue and how it affects so many areas of our society. I could tell, not just from this conversation but from many others that he was wrestling with different world views—the biblical world view he had grown up with, and the secular, humanistic world view he was getting from peers, school, and the media. I'll admit I was stretched on many occasions to defend just why I believed what I believed and to have evidence for it. It challenged me to take another look into my own views, but it did reinforce my own belief system. He had some very mind-provoking ideas and was not afraid to express them. I wanted desperately to keep that channel open. It was one way I could still express my love. The computer was now my major link to the son I was just really getting to know.

As I checked our email my heart jumped as my eyes landed on his name. I hoped it was an answer to the conversation we had started earlier in the week, this one being on how we had drifted apart. I opened the email.

"It's OK if you don't want to respond to this at all, but I thought I should say at least one more thing. I know you don't think I listen to you and take everything you say wrong, but I understand that I have hurt both you and Dad. I am sorry and I don't blame you for assuming the worst of everything I say and do. Those wounds won't heal quickly and you don't have to believe me when I say that I love you or when I tell you I'm a Christian. You can blow them off, but that doesn't change the truth. I'm sorry I can't be more to you, maybe someday, but time will tell."

He then changed the subject and went on to say, "Hey, do you think it would be possible for me to get a car and have it at least some of the time by your place? There was this awesome Subaru I thought was gonna work perfect but I walked by it earlier and it totally isn't, lol. I am so not gonna buy another Dinah . . . ya know?"

I responded, "Gee—did Dinah teach us something? lol." My mind went back to the Dinah episode.

He had been talking a lot about getting a car. After getting his license at sixteen he, like most teenagers, relished the freedom he now had. At seventeen, using Mom and Dad's car wasn't always convenient. However, we had told him from day one that we were not the kind of parents who would supply a teenage boy with a car. We had explained that if he wanted a car he would have to pay for it, as well as for the upkeep. If he would do that we would help out with the insurance. So he knew better than to ask us to buy him a car. Dad did, however, offer a suggestion.

"I'll make you an offer. You can buy our 1991 Corolla from me over time. You can make payments and we'll keep you on our insurance. It's still in good shape so you shouldn't have any maintenance on it," Gary explained, trying to make it as appealing as possible.

"Thanks, Dad, but I think I found one I like on Craigslist," Scott replied, hesitating only briefly.

"My goodness," I said, adding my two cents to the conversation "Dad's offer sounds like a good deal. Seems to me you sure do like driving it a lot, as you drive it almost as much as I do."

"But I found this really cool 1985 Volkswagen Beetle on Craigslist. It sounds super—only eight hundred dollars. Do you think we can check it out?" he asked excitedly. The more practical offer was now definitely off the table.

We inquired about his ability to pay. He said he had been saving up. No big surprise he had been saving, but we were surprised he had that much. Gary told him no matter what car he picked he had better get it checked out with Tom, our mechanic. He had done that for us on several occasions and we were glad, since it saved us a lot of money in future repairs. Scott promised he would and I went with him to assess the car.

Scott fell in love at first sight and I knew that could be trouble. There were times when he let his emotions overrule common sense and facts. I feared this would be one of those occasions. Looking at it, he saw a wonderful blue Volkswagen that was just made for him. I, on the other hand, saw a beat up, old, faded-blue car that needed more repairs than the ad had led us to believe. The interior didn't look good. The dashboard covering was torn and faded. All the knobs were either cracked or missing. Looking at the floorboards, I noticed they were thin and rusted, and the seat covers were intact but shabby. Besides, it smelled like cigarette smoke.

The whole thing made me nervous, but, Scott asked to take it for a test drive. Opening the door excitedly, he got in. It didn't start right away, which should have given him a clue as to its condition, and it sputtered as it left the driveway. As I stood waiting for him to come back, I wondered what option I should pursue. Option A, tell him that this was not the car he thought it was and tell him not to buy it. Or option B, let him make up his own mind and learn a life lesson. As he returned from his short drive, I knew I had to make up my mind. He pulled into the driveway and turned off the car. It sputtered again and clanked as it stopped.

"This is so cool, Mom!" he exclaimed as he jumped out of the car with his eyes dancing and face beaming.

As I looked over the car again and back to him I said, "How did it drive, though?"

The owner was a man in his early forties, rough shaven, rather rotund, and generally unkempt in appearance, with a demeanor that didn't hit me right. Shifting his feet from side to side, he was showing impatience. He cocked his head and gave several big sighs. Perhaps having a moment of conscience, he noted a minor repair. "Keep in mind; it does need a new oil pan."

When I heard that, I wondered what else there was to repair that he wasn't divulging.

"Hey, it ran great!" Scott beamed. He saw the look of doubt on my face.

My eyes darted to the well-worn tires, "Are you going to have Tom look at it?"

"I think it's OK." He continued to look at the car adoringly.

"Are you sure you want to spend all that money on this car?" I asked, hoping he would take another, more thorough look at this machine, given his unwillingness to part with money.

"Yeah, this is just what I want!" he said, gazing into my eyes, hoping to find approval.

"Well, it's your money and your decision," I said as I looked back at him, shrugging my shoulders and tilting my head. I had just gone with Option B, letting him make his own decision. It pained me somewhat since I knew what was in store. Life lessons are always difficult. But knowing him as I did I knew he wasn't going to learn any other way. The gentleman was standing by the garage door, arms crossed, smiling (or was it a smirk?) as he knew he had hooked a good one.

"Are you going to take it?" he asked rather rhetorically, as he couldn't help but overhear Scott's joyous tone during our conversation.

Scott looked at me with my resolute face, then back at the seller. "Yeah," he said, his tone changing a bit as reality hit. He now had to part with his cash. Pulling out his wad of cash, Scott started to count out eight hundred dollars as the man held out his hand. I thought, *My land, I would be sweating bullets if I had that much money at seventeen and gave it all away like that. I still would sweat bullets even now!*

The man filled out the paperwork and handed Scott the keys.

"It's yours. Have fun!" he said, stuffing the wad of bills in his pocket. He turned and walked back toward the garage.

I started toward my car and said, "Go ahead, it's yours now. I'll follow you home," still mystified that the whole transaction actually took place.

He got in, started it up, and backed out of the driveway. I cringed as I heard the gears grind and the engine sputter. It wasn't long before we both knew that the car wasn't in the greatest of shape.

He revved up the engine, got up speed going down the slight hill. All of a sudden I found my heart in my throat. At the bottom of this little hill was a major intersection. He was headed right for it when it appeared the brakes didn't work right. Smoke started coming out of the rear wheel wells, then his car swerved all over the road, totally out of control. It careened into the next lane and spun around before heading in the right direction back in his lane. Only by God's grace did he not hit anyone or anything. The ride home was much slower.

I knew he had taken full possession of this car when he named it Dinah. A week later we took Dinah to the Volkswagen shop to see what repairs needed to be done. My suspicions were correct, since the oil pan wasn't the only thing on this list of "minor" repairs. The engine was totally shot, the floorboards were nonexistent, the tires were totally worn, and a host of other minor repairs were needed. The mechanic said it wasn't worth fixing.

Scott insisted on driving the car until it just gave up. He made Dinah his "hippy" bug by painting it with big yellow flowers, peace symbols, slogans, and his nickname, Pookey. He did drive it a little while around town, until Dinah finally gave up the ghost. It died as he was heading to Seattle, never to chug again. He hitchhiked a ride back home. Getting a friend to drive him where the car had stalled, he retrieved his belongings and left it on the side of the road. Thus ended the saga of Dinah. But she taught him much in her short existence.

God was teaching me lessons as well. He was trying to get my attention through all these situations He was putting me through. Just like Scott needed to learn those lessons through painful experiences, God also had to put me through some agonizing circumstances to teach me about trusting Him fully. I had not yet learned that *He* was in total control.

Chapter 12

MIXED BLESSINGS

I have come to have much joy
and comfort in your love
Philemon 7a (NASB)

I had just finished reading *The Shack*. Scott and I hadn't done much face-to-face communicating lately so I thought sharing this book would be a good way to connect. The book describes our relationship with God on a personal level and I thought it might strike a chord with him. I wanted to get a better understanding of where he was spiritually. His attendance at any church was nonexistent and his Bible reading was sporadic, at best. So I had a few questions for him.

I emailed him. "Hey—would you like to meet for dinner some night? I've got a book that might interest you."

"Sure—how about Panda Express at Cascade Station?" he wrote back.

"Works for me—see you at 6:30." I was excited first of all to see him again and also excited that he was willing to meet, since he probably figured I had ulterior motives with the book. I so looked forward to our meeting.

I arrived first. Searching out a booth toward the back of the restaurant, I sat down. As I looked at the buffet I was reminded of the several times we had eaten at these places as a family. It was his favorite restaurant. Gary and I enjoyed it but not as much as Scott. My mind drifted to a happier time and I began to smile. He walked in and my heart leapt; it was wonderful to see him. He had on his cat hat with the ears, bunches of brown hair showing underneath. His black hip-length jacket looked a little more worn than the last time I had seen it. But the jeans with the holes in the knees were the same. Catching my eye, he smiled, and came over to give me a hug. Oh, those hugs! So precious! How I missed them! Sitting across from each other, I began the dialogue.

"Hey! How's it going?" I asked. "How's work?" I continued, trying to warm up the conversation.

"It's OK. Getting up early to get the Max—can't count on it running on time in this cold weather," he explained. "The boss has been OK—I really like the other girls working there," he added pulling off his jacket. As he said "other girls" he looked at me a little harder to catch my reaction. I kept calm. I was glad he had found a job and was continuing to be conscientious about getting to work on time. He was working at one of the airport restaurants and enjoying the experience.

"Sounds good, at least you're getting there and still working. Hey, let's get some food," I said as I started to move toward the edge of the booth. "Take what you want, it's on me."

We got up from the table and went through the line. It all smelled so good but my mind wasn't on the food. He loaded up his plate. Upon being seated, I said a blessing for the food as I bowed my head. Reluctantly, he closed his eyes while I prayed a short prayer.

I wanted to get right to the point.

"I told you I got this book, *The Shack*. I'd like you to read it. Just one thing; don't take it as a theological study. You know enough of that," I remarked as we started to eat. I wanted to make my purpose clear. "What I'd like you to do is just put yourself in this guy's place and feel what he's going through. Try to grasp the relationship he starts to establish with God, the personal interaction they begin to have." I put my fork down and looked at him with sincerity.

He continued to eat but did not lift his eyes to meet mine.

I continued, coming more to the point.

"Remember how we talked before about our own relationship with God? I said each person's is unique—that's why it's personal. Yours is going to be different than mine but . . . "

Cutting me off and looking at me intently, he said emphatically, "Are you afraid I'm not a believer, Mom? If you are, don't worry, I am." He resumed eating. I didn't.

I smiled and pushed further. "I just want to make sure you know for sure. You fall into the same category I was. I grew up in a Christian home and felt I was a Christian just because my parents were."

"Mom, I remember when I made that decision," he said sternly, putting his fork to the side and looking at me.

"You do?"

"Yes, when I was in Sunday School with you. You don't think I remember?"

"Well, you were young and I've heard so many kids say they really don't remember making the decision after being told they had."

"Well, I do," he said, sounding slightly perturbed at my questions. Picking up his fork, he resumed eating his dinner.

Leaning back in my seat, I took comfort in knowing this. Our conversation seemed to be going well. I changed the subject and started making small talk about Dad and what was going on at home. He was attempting to clean the garage again. Since this was an ongoing thing with Dad, Scott let out a little chuckle at the thought. His last bites of orange chicken were now gone. We both put our forks on the plates and stood up to go.

Hugging him tightly, I told him, "I love you."

"Love you, too, Mom," he answered as he hugged back.

I watched him go out the door into the cold, wrapping his collar around his neck. I watched as he crossed the street to the Max station. Going out the door, I kept my eyes glued on him as I walked toward the car. I saw him sit down on the station bench. The light was shining on his head, with the cat-ears hat and the straggling hair, waiting for the Max that would take him back to downtown Portland, where he was living. I wanted to see the last little bit of him but couldn't bear to watch him leave so I got into my car. Putting my head down on the steering wheel, I felt the tears as his words rang in my head, "Love you, too, Mom."

My journal entry from that night:

Scott and I had our dinner date. I haven't prayed so much about one thing in a long time—I was so apprehensive. But I found out what I wanted to—he knows he has made a decision for Christ and I just challenged him to get to know Him better. I felt so inadequate as I had to choose my words so carefully. We talked for two hours. I miss our chats—when I could ask him questions freely, without feeling guarded. As I looked at him tonight I was looking forward to getting to know him growing into manhood. I'm sure one day God will put the pieces together from all those shattered dreams.

Chapter 13

SOME QUESTIONS ANSWERED

Without consultation, plans are frustrated,
But with many counselors they succeed.
Proverbs 15:22 (NASB)

I still had many questions regarding this whole transgender issue. I had heard so many conflicting opinions. I was still confused about what it is, where it comes from, and, of course, was there any help for it. My search for answers ramped up.

My journal entry:

His last emails sounded confused but Jim says that's the way it is—the whole Gender Identity Disorder thing is very confusing to those who are in it. Scott's also asking about my past. I have been open and honest about what I had gone through growing up as a "tomboy" and wanting to be a boy. I hope and pray I continue to convey what God would have me say regarding this and continue to direct our conversations. I still have to really force myself to say the strongest things and not just "skirt" around the issues. I still doubt myself in what I say and my responses to his remarks. Still hoping I can make a difference yet realizing there's only so much I can do as far as my part is concerned. Oh, God—use my words and humble attempts from a mom who wants her son back.

I reached out for anything and to anybody who could shed some light. I got in touch with Harold from a Christian ministry dealing with transgender issues. I explained my situation via email and we had quite a few exchanges. I told him my biggest concerns at the moment were: (1) Scott felt we were making the situation worse as he felt it was his choice and only affected him; (2) Scott felt as his parents we should have been supportive of him and accepted him as God accepted him.

There was another question I didn't ask, and I'm not sure why. Maybe it was because I didn't think it should be asked or maybe because I was just afraid. Just another one of those nagging doubts going through my head. However, he did address it and I'm glad he did. Since he had done a lot of research in this area, he mentioned that transgender is not genetically linked, nor does it have any physiological origins in the brain. Therefore, it is psychological in nature. There was my answer. I just had to have affirmation.

One thing he mentioned really hit me. He said that we as Christians want very simple, single-handed solutions. We expect God to make things "all better" very quickly. So, he said, be patient. Try not to be confrontational. Be understanding in conversations and try to see how Scott has come to think this way. He also reminded me of some theological points.

Scott has been profoundly influenced by the world's system of thinking. His decisions are based on wrong thinking, which will always lead to sin. He will make his own choices. God will allow him to do this as part of His permissive will. And I needed to keep in mind I cannot control what he will choose. That was not so easy to do, as I had discovered. When I tried to be understanding, he would almost always turn it into a confrontation.

Harold mentioned that many therapists have concluded it *is* biological and therefore are "fast tracking" individuals through to surgery. This was most discouraging. This opinion fueled Scott's decision since he was getting his information from the Internet. After reading Harold's emails, I felt as if I had opened up a door and was starting down a long hallway that I didn't want to walk down. It was so complicated! A whole community of "experts" was working against us. Immediate and personal help, it seemed, was not forthcoming.

But I kept the communication going. I told him how much I appreciated his insight and reiterated that God would be the ultimate healer in this situation. I wanted to know, however, if Gary and I had done all we could to restore him. I had a couple of questions that were still nagging at me. Should we present Scott with this new information, that is, the articles and research? More important and more pressing, though, how could we continue to show our love for him without supporting his actions? Unfortunately, I told him, Scott associated our love with our support (or lack thereof). We were groping for answers in an area where we had no clue but were trusting God to see us through.

The support issue he expressed was just the tip of the iceberg. Underneath, I sensed Scott was in emotional turmoil, as I was. I was torn in so many ways. Because Scott thought support equaled love, I felt my love was being held hostage. We repeatedly told him that we loved him unconditionally but his snappy response as always was, "Sure, love the sinner, hate the sin."

Harold affirmed that we were being manipulated by Scott even though we tried tough love and confrontation.

I shared with Harold the conversation we had had with the high school principal.

"In our discussion, the principal made it very clear that this decision affects other people, not just Scott. Scott's argument is that it is his decision and everyone should accept that. He's also convinced himself that becoming a woman is the only solution. To use his words, 'There's only two ways I'm coming out of this—as a woman or in a body bag.' On one hand I am discouraged because of his attitude and my total inadequacy at handling his arguments but on the other hand I have to know that God is still working. 'His grace is sufficient.'"

I continued to research. Along with more research confirming there is no biological confirmation, other findings struck me. The opinion that this disorder is going to be more prevalent in the coming years among young people was disturbing. Caitlin Ryan, in an article entitled, "Hope in a World of Gender Confusion" quotes Devon Williams and Jeff Johnson,

"I think the fluidity of gender is the next big wave in terms of adolescent development. Gender has become part of the defining way that youth organize themselves and rebel against adults."

They go on to say that even though transsexuals may have surgery, it doesn't change the fact they are still the biological sex they were born with; it's in every cell of their body. Surgery may change the outward appearance, but it cannot change the underlying biological reality.

This was what Gary and I had been constantly trying to get across to Scott. You can think all you want, change all you want, but you will never change who God made you to be. It will always be with you and it will forever color everything you do from that point on.

After reading one of Harold's articles, I thought back to some earlier talks with Scott. Harold noted that *envy* was the primary root of this lifestyle.

I was particularly struck that this totally described Scott. From our conversations, and from an observation of one of his counselors, it seemed that he *wished* he were a girl. Oh, he would catch himself from time to time to make his point and say he *knew* he was a girl. But because of this, I felt it was so very important we get help before he did make any permanent change. I knew deep down that this was *not* the solution to his dilemma. Nevertheless, I felt we were on a time clock, each day a tick closer to his life as a woman or in a body bag. I also knew that each day we had him there was the hope of redemption.

Chapter 14

UNEXPECTED EVENTS

God is our refuge and strength,
abundantly available
for help in tight places.
Psalm 46:1

Courts are a hodgepodge of all sorts of people—good people who have made bad decisions and bad people who have done bad things. Seeing families here with their younger children, I'm wondering if these kids will one day find themselves in this courtroom as they watch their brothers or uncles or fathers appear. Other people belong here but I don't. I'm sitting here trying to be supportive of my son, who finally got caught doing something he knew was wrong. He's used to getting away with doing wrong things since he's had a lot of practice. We've lived through his lying and deceit and that has, unfortunately, hardened my heart.

This episode started five days ago when we got "the call," you know, the one every parent of a teenager hopes they never get and dreads when it happens; "Dad, I'm in jail."

Like most parents, we had told him if you get arrested you're doing the time. His next words anticipated our reaction. "I don't expect you to bail me out, just wanted to let you know." He said he wasn't at liberty to say anything yet, so we didn't ask any further questions. Oh, wow. He'd gone and done it this time. I could only imagine what he was going through. As I found out later, I *couldn't* imagine.

Since he was in for several days, he made another call, asking if I would call his boss and tell her he wouldn't be in to work and that he would work things out with her later. He also told us when his court date was and ended the conversation with a desperate plea to please let him come back home. He would do anything we asked.

Gary and I were pretty nervous as we approached the courthouse on the appointed day. It was the first time we had been in a courtroom. This was not TV, where you can change the channel when you get tired of the drama. Everything was all too real. The deputy watched everything from the sideline with his gun on his side. The judge was in his black robe, sitting high on his bench, looking at the papers in front of him, then peering over his glasses at the people before him waiting anxiously for his decision. When Scott's name was called, I strained to see him come from the holding room. I wondered what he would look like after several days in jail. My heart was pierced as I saw him make his way to the bench.

He looked pretty shaken up. He wore the jailhouse orange jumpsuit with CLARK COUNTY JAIL printed on the back, his hands and feet shackled, his hair totally disheveled, his sandals barely covering his feet. Then I also noticed the one item that was missing—his bra. This must have been the most devastating for him. My heart pounded inside me. I was ripped in two pieces. My mind was telling me, *I hope this serves as a wake-up call so things will start to change.* My heart was telling me, *He's still my son, even if he's a criminal.* I've never seen him so humble as he stood there motionless before the judge, head bowed. He always knew how to act to his advantage, but I sensed he truly was scared. He had told us in one of our conversations that he was arrested for stealing some clothes and that they were making a big deal out of it. However, we started to wonder a bit when the judge put the bail at $25,000. Could that be for a simple trespassing and burglary charge? The judge noticed he had no permanent address as he had been living at a teen shelter in Portland for the past several months. He therefore asked if anyone was with him whom he could be released to. Scott told him his parents were there. Gary and I looked at each other, totally taken aback. I do remember standing up, not knowing what else we could do but also not knowing what we were in for. His court-appointed lawyer motioned for us to talk with him for a moment. I thought to myself, *Oh, yes, please! Explain what is happening! Twenty-five thousand dollars bail?*

The bottom line to the conversation with the attorney was that if we took him in our custody the charge would be reduced; otherwise, he would remain in jail for a full sentence on a felony charge. We had no idea a felony charge would be an option and were stunned, totally unprepared to take him back into our home. My mind was spinning. *What would it mean for him to have a felony record? Would it really be best for him to serve more jail time? Does he* **expect** *us to do this for him? After all he's put us through, I'm going to take him back?* A decision! We had to tell the judge *now.*

Since it would only be for a short time until the next court date, we agreed to take him back with us. My mother's heart was silently whispering, *No matter what you've done, no matter who you are, you are still my son and I love you. I wish with all my heart I could make it all better for you.*

When I picked him up from jail, all he said was that he "wanted to get the hell out of there." He didn't say thanks for picking him up, didn't show appreciation for anything, didn't apologize for anything as he hopped in the truck. He told me a little bit about his time there. He said they really didn't know where to put him, so they put him in the psych ward, which, he admitted, was scary. Because he was transgender, they couldn't keep him in the men's ward as a woman but since he was still male, they couldn't put him in the women's ward. What really upset him was that they made him take off his bra.

Since he was now in our custody and at home, he had to clear out his things from transitional housing. When he first mentioned his "trans" housing, I immediately assumed it was specifically for transgendered people. But that wasn't the case. It was an apartment complex in the heart of Portland run by the city for young people, up to the age of twenty-one, transitioning from living on the streets. He later told me he had been on the streets for a short time before coming to the trans housing. I was glad I hadn't known that earlier. I would have been so worried about him. He had told me he had been living with other kids but this was the first time I actually saw the place. He definitely liked it there, in the middle of town, close to all the action with easy access to public transportation, which made it easy getting to work.

Finding a parking space for the truck near the building was a chore. I had driven him there as Gary was otherwise occupied and others were waiting to get into his room. We finally found a parking space, fortunately, close to the door. He got out as soon as we parked. I opened my door.

"Mom, you have to stay here. They won't let anybody over twenty-one in the rooms," he explained as he closed the door and headed toward the building.

Emerging from the building with his arms full, I began to wonder just how much paraphernalia he had accumulated. In this load there was a big stuffed tiger, several pillows, a large dog bed, a couple of blankets, and a load of clothes.

"How much stuff do you have?" I began to wonder if we shouldn't have rented a larger van for this escapade.

"Hey, I've been here for a while. Do your magic thing and pack it all in," he remarked as he left the items by the curb. Turning around, he went back for more. Thank goodness most of the items were crushable and malleable, easy to squeeze into the limited space. As he brought load after load, I continued to pile everything in, pushing and shoving into every available cranny.

"Is that it?" I asked, slightly out of breath.

"Oh, can't forget my bike," he said turning toward the rack where it was stored.

We both grabbed a side and lifted it up and over all the piles and managed to get it in, then climbed in and closed the doors. I was apprehensive about the ride home but decided to open the conversation.

"How was your stay here?" I questioned, hoping to start on a positive note.

"It was pretty cool. We had to make our own meals and I even made blueberry pancakes, like you make at home. Everybody thought they were great," he answered in an upbeat tone. "Dinners were pretty sketchy, but we did OK."

"Did they work with you in any way, give you help with getting other housing or jobs?" I queried.

"Yeah, that's the whole idea of this thing. They give you some places to check out for jobs then you have to go and talk to them, then come back and fill out a report. You have to go through their little hoops but I did get that job at the airport through them, so I guess it works." He started to relax in the seat, putting his feet up on the dashboard. "But you have to be out by the time you're twenty-one."

I didn't want to go too deeply into what he had done there, fearful of getting into a confrontation. It was small talk for the rest of the drive home. I also didn't want to think about what the next weeks would bring. It would be a strain. Coming back under our authority was not something he relished. However, he knew it was his only option. However, that didn't keep him from pushing the boundaries as he had before. His second court appearance was four weeks later.

Here we sit again but this time he sits with us. His name was called and he went forward, as he did before, politely addressing the judge. Ultimately, the judge put him in the "diversion program" and he got off with probation for six months and a few other stipulations. As he stood in front of the large desk, he cocked his head and shifted his weight to one side, relaxing his stance. I could sense he was probably thinking he would eventually get around the probation issue as well. However, he still had to come back in six weeks for another court date. We never did learn the real truth in this matter. We figured it wasn't worth the discussion it would foster. In the meantime, he continued to stay with us. We were not looking forward to that.

Our time as a family- and I use the term loosely- had not been pleasant in any way that last year, especially the last several months. We had lost our family connection, as his transgender issue had loosened those bonds we once enjoyed. That was the knife constantly in my heart. Each time we argued or found out something he had done behind our backs, or said something destructive about us, the knife twisted a little more. How much could I bleed? At night as I lay in my bed I would hear him clicking away on his laptop in his room, messaging his friends or accessing who-knows-what website to look up the best way and place to get his surgery done. I cried in my pillow until it was soaked with my tears. *God, do you hear me? All I wanted was a simple family—the three of us enjoying one another, laughing, caring about one another. Was that too much to ask? What am I doing wrong? I don't KNOW what to do! God, you're not giving me any answers! Are you hearing me?!*

Sleep was only a temporary respite, since each morning came with new anxieties. It took all I could muster to remember God was in control, but trusting in His ways was becoming more and more difficult. I kept reading scriptures and books about scripture and books about people going through difficulties, but it was so hard to see "the good in all things" (Romans 8:28) at that point. I did have moments of "casting my cares on Him" (I Peter 5:7) and that release was uplifting, but truly those moments were few and far between. My journey to "counting it all joy" (James 1:2) had taken a definite detour.

Scott did go back to work. He was working at the Portland airport and apparently doing well at his job, getting good reviews from the reports he had shown me. Now that he was with us we told him he would be responsible to get himself up and to work every day. He needed this job desperately so he would do anything to keep it. It was still quite cold in the mornings, but he rode his bike the six or so miles to the airport, get there by five o'clock, and ride back after work. I truly admired him for that. It reminded me of the mornings he would get up early to go shopping with me. Once again, it proved that he really could do something if he wanted it badly enough—which also made me scared. He wanted his transition surgery very badly and as soon as he could get the money he was going to do it. That's why this job was so important to him. God thwarted those plans, however, in a big way.

Scott had been late for work a couple of days and if he was late again, he would lose his job. His schedule changed from week to week and he was always careful to check to see before leaving work when he needed to come in the next few days.

He was home just preparing to leave (he was working later that day) when he got a phone call from his boss asking where he was. He said he was on his way. Apparently, he had gotten the time wrong from the sheet and was supposed to be there an hour before he thought. From this last mistake he lost his job. With that mistake he lost the possibility of getting the rest of the money he needed for the procedure. I could only imagine what emotions he was feeling. My first thought was, *God, you have something in mind and I'm hoping it will give him more time to think about what he's doing.* Unfortunately, time can be a cruel thing as it can turn our world upside down in one second but make our world a prison, holding us captive the next. Seconds pass into minutes and minutes into hours. Time most assuredly kept Scott in its grasp as those hours turned into painful days. He kept thinking about how to turn his world right side up when he didn't know which side was up.

Several weeks later, I was in the back room on the computer. The week before, I had found out he had scheduled a "gender reassignment" surgery. It was planned to take place in Thailand, in four months. Scott sauntered in and stood by my shoulder. Giving me his best smile and soothing voice, he bent down by my head and said, "You want me to be happy, right?"

Oh, no, I thought. *This is not good. What does he want me to do now?* My mind raced to all sorts of places, none where I wanted to go. *He's going to put me in an awkward position, so I'd better be careful with my answer.*

"Ye-e-s," I responded slowly and carefully.

"Well, you know this operation is going to make me happy. Do you think you and Dad could give me a loan for the rest of the money I need?" he asked, still calm but deliberate.

"We've told you whatever you do from here is on your own," I told him. I didn't want to sound frustrated or put out. There might be an opening for a discussion.

I got up from my chair and sat on the edge of the pool table where he had now planted himself. I looked at him with a concerned but soft look; I didn't want to come across as if I were lecturing. I crossed my legs, leaned forward on my arms, took a little sigh, and began.

"Before you do anything, I want you to consider some things. I know you've done a lot of thinking and I know you think this is going to be the best thing to make you happy. But here's the deal. First of all, you're having this done in a foreign country where you will be all by yourself. Do you know where you're going? Who's going to take care of you over there? You'll need a place to recover after the surgery. Where will you go?"

"They have all that arranged," he said, quick with the answer. "They have a room included in the price." This was supposed to put my mind at ease. But I continued.

"Well suppose something goes wrong? There's always the risk of infection—so what if you have to stay longer and have additional care? This is major surgery—irreversible surgery, I might add. You're still a teenager. What if you decide later that this wasn't right?"

"Oh, I know this is right. Most people who have this done later in life say they should have done it sooner; they wasted time," he explained as he continued to look at me. His manner and voice conveyed he was still open for talk. Crisscrossing his legs, he relaxed his shoulders and spoke softly but firmly. He wanted me to know he had done his homework and had the answers. I had more questions.

"You don't have a job right now. How are you going to manage when you get home? You're going to have to have a place to live and an income. Do you think you can get a job right away? And relationships. That's a whole other matter. If you get serious about a guy are you going to tell him sooner or later that you're trans? It's going to affect you in a lot of other ways besides physical appearance. All your dad and I want you to do is take your time. Get your life together—find out what you want to do other than this surgery. Get your education and a job." As I was looking at him with as much sincerity and love as I could communicate, he was looking back with doubt and confusion. I continued.

"I know you're bent on getting it done right away but there are so many things to take into account that I don't think you've thought about. Just wait a bit. That's all we want you to do. Take your time—you've got your whole life ahead of you." Our eyes locked, searching each other for some common ground on which to agree. Long silence.

"So, I guess you won't give me the money," he finally said firmly, standing up, turning around, and walking away. I hung my head as my prayer went heavenward, *Oh, Lord, help him understand this will not bring him the happiness he wants. He's still young and has so much ahead of him. Protect my baby.*

Chapter 15

BITTERSWEET FAREWELL

I know that you can do all things;
no plan of yours can be thwarted.
Job 42:2

Scott was still serving his probation time, keeping him close to home. Having no job meant he was spending major portions of the day with us. All in all, we all dealt with the situation pretty well. No blowups and no heated arguments had taken place. But it was only a lull before the storm.

The days were getting longer. The weather was warming up, flowers were flourishing, and attitudes were perking up. It was for most of us. Scott's attitude wasn't the perkiest at one point since he had a chore to do. The big spruce tree in the front of the house had left a lot of small needles and general tree debris on the roof. Gary wasn't up to the task of getting up on the roof and sweeping all that debris. I had done it before but we both agreed that Scott needed to be doing more around the house. He was able, not necessarily willing.

"Scott, I need you to go up on the roof to sweep off the mess from under that tree," Gary told him. When time had passed and he hadn't made much movement off the couch toward the roof, the order was given with a little more emphasis. "Get up on that roof like I told you—NOW!" Gary barked as he pointed to the door. His patience wearing thin, he turned around, shaking his head, and headed back toward his study.

"All right, I'm going—geez, don't get all huffy. What broom do you want me to use?" he asked as he put down his laptop and started moving slowly off the couch.

"Use the old one in the garage. Get the ladder out and be careful getting up there," Gary told him as he returned to his studying. Saturday afternoons were Gary's time for preparing Sunday's message. He peeked around the corner just to make sure there was follow-up this time.

"Yeah, sure," Scott replied as he started slowly toward the garage. He made it very obvious this was not one of his favorite Saturday afternoon chores.

Doing my chores on the lawn, I would look up on the roof from time to time as I passed by. Occasionally he would push the broom around the needles and some would fall off the roof. At other times I saw him swaying to the music on his iPod, mouthing the words, using the broom as a microphone or guitar. Although I couldn't hear the tunes I imagined he was listening to Pink Floyd or the Beatles, his favorites, although he listened to a wide selection of artists. I realized it was a mundane chore so I didn't get on his case. Some distraction was certainly allowed. I continued about my own mundane chore picking up tree debris and raking up small branches that had been strewn about on the lawn from the latest windstorm. After some time had passed, I noticed he had accomplished much of the cleaning and was just sitting on his haunches, twirling the broom.

"Why don't you come on down and we can do something?" I suggested, since I felt like doing something different myself. He didn't put up much of a fuss, just shrugged and started down the ladder. In the meantime, I spotted the basketball out by the hoop belonging to the neighbors across the street, free-standing at the edge of their driveway. It had been put up years ago when the boys were young and it had certainly served its purpose. Apparently, someone had been playing recently and left the ball out. So as Scott came out to the street, I tossed him the ball. Without putting down his broom, he swooshed the broom underneath the ball and flipped the ball toward the basket. Well, that gave me an idea.

"Wait here. I'll be back in a second," I told him as I hurried off toward the house.

"Since *you* have a broom, I can use one, too," I said as I came back to the basket with a broom in my hand. Hence, a game of broom basketball ensued. It was rather tricky as you had to dribble and shoot using only the broom. There was a lot of swatting and batting as we both tried to gain control and keep possession of the ball. The hardest part was trying to get the broom underneath the ball while still maintaining enough balance of the ball to lift it up and loft it into the basket.

"Hey! You actually made it in!" I yelled.

"Maybe we can make this a new sport," he said as he laughed at me trying to gain control of the ball as it started rolling down the street, my broom waving wildly.

"I think we need to perfect our technique," I said, my voice trailing as I ran after the errant ball. A little out of breath, I came back to the basket, dribbling the ball with my broom. He immediately went into action to try to steal it away.

"Good grief," I panted. "Give me a break!"

"Ha—you don't give *me* any breaks!" he shot back. This went on for an hour or more, laughing and commenting on our antics as we tried to perfect different broom techniques.

That was the last fun time we spent together.

He left shortly afterward to go back to live in Portland. The hoop is now gone since the neighbors have moved. But the sweet memories remain. Even now when I look at the old broom in the garage I'm reminded of the silliness, the laughter, and the friendly competition we enjoyed that day playing broom basketball.

I particularly relish this memory because it was a respite during a very troubled time. He had been at home since his last court date, almost six weeks previous. However, the dynamics in our family had started to change for the worse. The tension had been steadily increasing, especially the last couple of weeks. He was talking more about his transition, being more antagonistic toward us, and very antisocial. He would stay in his room for days at a time without speaking. We would reach out by trying to include him in some activity or at least start a conversation but it was very clear that his time at home was coming to an end. I was becoming more concerned about his overall mental state as the time he had proposed for his transition had come and gone. He realized he needed to make other plans for living arrangements, but I wasn't sure what he had in mind. He just said he was going to stay with friends since he couldn't go back to the teen transition house in Portland. We agreed on a date of departure. When the day came he took a few things in his backpack and rode off on his bicycle. That was right before Mother's Day weekend. The entry in my journal reads:

> "I was spending Mother's Day with Mom because I couldn't bear being here with reminders of that day. I knew Scott would do nothing to remember the day. It would have been a very vivid reminder of a relationship gone badly. As it turned out he left shortly after I did. Gary said he didn't leave mad or angry or upset. It was our request he leave but all of us have come to the breaking point. Gary is so much more relaxed. But it's like when Scott left the first time—I still anticipate him being here, I smell his particular smell, I think what he would like to eat. He's got his court date this week and I'll admit I'm anxious. I gave him a name of a counselor that I would pay for but if he has any encouragement he'll be off for Thailand before long. That is a constant pain in my mind but also a constant reminder that I have to trust God in the "even if" situation. 'Be still (my soul) and know that I am God.'"

We would hear from him from time to time but he wouldn't tell us exactly where he was. He would email a bit as well but it wasn't the same as before. I missed the communication we had; I wondered where he was, if he was eating enough, who he was with, if he was safe. My heart yearned and ached to know about my child, yet I knew if I did know I would probably ache even more. I had to deal with the fact that he was making his own decisions, right or wrong, and I had to abide by them. I had to take him out of his mother's care and leave him totally in his Heavenly Father's love. Everything was truly out of my control.

He dropped by the house a week later when I wasn't home. Gary said he had come by to get the truck. I was surprised Gary had given him the keys on several accounts.

"How was he?" I inquired, anxious to hear.

"He was very nice, seemed upbeat and happy—actually had a good conversation."

"Well that's good," I said, relaxing a bit. I turned away, sighing. I could feel my shoulders dropping as the tension started to leave. Then I turned back around and asked, "Did you ask him what he needed it for?"

"He said he needed it to haul a few things since he was moving to a different place to live," he answered matter-of-factly. Then he added hesitantly, "He asked for a hug and told me he loved me. We hugged and I told him I loved him, too. Took me a little off-guard," he admitted.

It was the last time they embraced.

"Did you ask him when he would bring it back?" Now I was getting nervous. Scott had a history with the truck. He had wrecked it once and also had a habit of not letting us know exactly what he was doing with it or where he was going.

"I told him, 'Just don't take it to Seattle.' He said he wouldn't and said he would bring it back in a few days, when he was done," Gary shrugged. The whole conversation didn't seem to bother him at all.

I *was* concerned, especially as I got to thinking he didn't have anything to move that required a truck; many of his things were still here. This kept gnawing at me but I rationalized he could have acquired some pieces of furniture. Those doubts kept troubling me. I couldn't imagine what use he could have in mind for the truck. But my concern was well-founded. It wasn't long before I found out his true intent. It wasn't good.

Chapter 16

FATEFUL END

When I am afraid, I will put my trust in Thee.
Thou hast taken account of my wanderings;
Put my tears in Thy bottle; are they not in Thy book?
Psalm 56:3,8 (NASB)

Friday, June 5, 2009. Just another date on the cal-
endar; just another Friday evening. Another workout, another
night just like any other—or so I thought. This Friday would
be like no other. It would be burned into my memory like a hot
branding iron sears the hide.

I had just returned from a workout at the gym, putting my
body through another punishing workout with the weights.
Gary and I work out together on Fridays, and we had done so
this Friday, but for some reason we had taken two cars. I had
finished my workout; Gary was taking it a bit slower so I had
come home early to get dinner ready. That would be a welcome

change since we usually ate late, about nine o'clock, and it was only about seven o'clock. But before I started dinner, I sat down at the computer, to chill just a bit and wind down. Still in my workout clothes and a bit sweaty, I started to check our emails. I took a long sigh of relaxation, stretched out my legs, took a few sips of water and began the task at hand. It seemed as if I had been there just moments and had started to relax when I heard the doorbell. *Humm,* I thought, *who could that be? I'm certainly not expecting anybody and whoever it is I hope they don't stay; I'm not in the mood for conversation or visitors.* I peered through the glass eyehole in the door and noticed it was a police officer. *Oh, no,* I thought, *here we go again; what had Scott done now?* My head raced to think what it might be as my heart started to beat a bit faster. I made up my mind I wasn't going to get involved in whatever mischief Scott may have been in but my mind immediately went into overdrive trying to think what it could possibly be. *Did he steal something? Did he hit something with the truck? Was he in an accident? Is he all right?* As I opened the door to speak with him, I tried to look as nonchalant as I could, given it was a police officer looking at me in my sweaty clothes.

He began to speak, with a question.

"Do you know where your son is?" he asked with no emotion.

What do you mean, "Do you know where your son is?" I thought. *Why would I know where he is? He hasn't lived here for several weeks. You must know more than I if you're here asking about him.*

"No, I haven't seen him lately," I answered. "He said he might apply for a job at the Cinetopia, the theater around the corner, so you might check to see if he's working there. He has our truck so you might keep your eye out for the big white van. Other than that, I couldn't tell you."

"OK, thank you," he said, with no variance in his voice. Then he turned around and left. I just stood there for a moment and thought, *That was pretty random.* I had no idea why a police officer would come and ask very calmly where my son was. There was no sense of urgency in his voice, no blinking lights, or anything that would mean an emergency situation so I decided to go back to the computer, albeit a bit confused. It surely had to be something to do with the truck.

I couldn't concentrate and it occurred to me to check out the Cinetopia. Not really sure why, other than curiosity, to see if he had, indeed, gotten a job there and was working. I knew it was a long shot but I had to see for myself. Since it was just down the street, it was no big deal to walk down. So I put my shoes back on. Thinking I would be right back, I didn't change my clothes, sweaty as they were. I walked out the door into the cool night air and as I started to walk the short distance more and more thoughts came into my head—not the best of thoughts, either. Then my neighbor, who lives in a corner house, across from the theater, came out of her house and approached me as I advanced toward her driveway. Her hands were in her pockets and she had this "look." Then I knew something was terribly wrong. My heart was now beating out of my chest—this couldn't be good. My neighbor didn't walk with me as I picked up the pace. As I came to the end of the block and started to make the turn around the corner, I noticed people gathered around the parking lot. *What are they doing just standing around?* They were looking across the parking lot; some were still holding their drinks as they had just come out of the theater, some just had their hands over their mouths. I couldn't see down the length of the parking lot because of bushes in the way. As soon as I turned the corner my eyes spotted our big white truck at the far end, in the corner slot right under the theater marquee and a street light. A midsized white van with CORONER in bold, black letters on the back was parked immediately behind it. Right then my world came to an end.

I seemed to be looking at a black and white photograph, with nobody moving and everybody looking at that van and our very large truck. There was the pudgy coroner with his emblazoned jacket MEDICAL EXAMINER; there was his assistant in a blue jacket, indicating they were both from the county office. People stood by their cars, looking. There were even some people stopped on the sidewalk. It had been a nice summer night with a slight breeze but there was no movement in the trees. People weren't moving. Cars weren't passing by. Time had again swept me into its clutches. ***Please, rewind,*** my mind yelled inside me, *to the way things were, even as bad as they seemed to be.* ***I don't want to be in this moment!*** But time grabs you and you become its slave. Then it was no longer a still shot. It became fast motion.

NO! At that moment I wanted to be anywhere other than that place, looking at that sight, knowing what the inevitable outcome would be. I started running to the parking lot, but a police officer, oddly the same one who had come to the house, stopped me and told me very straightforwardly, "Your son is dead." I looked into his eyes. They were emotionless. *That's it? My son is dead? No "I'm sorry" or anything else to say you might feel a little of my pain? Are you that uncaring?*

With nowhere else to go, faint, and numb, I slumped into his arms and sobbed uncontrollably, ***"MY BABY'S GONE!"*** My heart was yelling, *God! You took my baby! Did you have to take him? He's my only son!*

I now noticed who was in the crowd of people who had gathered; some were patrons of the theater, others were perhaps classmates who had known him since he was only a year out of high school. How could *they* know all about this before me, his mother? I felt intruded upon, invaded. I wanted to shout "Get away. Let me be with my son!" But I didn't. The officer offered to sit with me in his car for some privacy while we waited for Gary. I knew he would be by soon and would see the crowd, as well as me, as he passed by the theater to turn the corner to the house. We sat there for a few minutes and I told him immediately that I was OK, that I knew my son was in heaven, face-to-face with his Savior, Jesus Christ.

After a short time, Gary drove up and I jumped out of the police car. I ran to Gary and as he stepped out of the car I cried out, "Scott's gone." His reaction was the same as mine. "Face-to-face with Jesus," he said sadly as we embraced in each other's arms. We both cried for a brief time, just holding on to each other, each looking to the other for comfort and for someone to say, "It will be OK," when we both knew it wouldn't.

We then made our way to the coroner's truck. The coroner met us before we got there and told us it would be best not to see the body. Because Scott had used helium as his method of suicide it had turned the skin a greenish hue. He also said that his death was very painless and quick. Yes, that was my son— did his research to know the best way to go. The officers said it looked like he had been living in the truck for some time. My emotions were turned upside down. Hurt mixed with anger, mixed with pity, and my mother's protecting love as I thought of what he must have gone through, living in the truck. *Why? Where were your "friends?" Where were we? You didn't deserve this.* The coroner told us they were not going to do an autopsy, since it looked clear-cut there was no foul play.

The chaplains came and asked if there was anything they could do to help; we just smiled politely and thanked them for their concern and assured them we knew God was in control. We knew they were just doing their job, but what could they do? We were at peace, knowing assuredly that our son was enjoying an embrace by his Savior, free of the pain he had been in these last few years. They weren't going to change anything and God had provided His word in our hearts and minds for such an occasion as this. We had no idea then what journey God would take us on through the ensuing years because of this one moment in time, but we had to trust He knew what He was doing.

I remember thinking that God answered my "worst prayer." Scott had said several times, "If I can't live my life as a woman, I don't want to live it at all" and because of his previous attempt, I prayed if that day would ever come, that God would allow him to be found.

At this point the numbness began to set in. My mind was not thinking; my body was going through motions. What now? Well, we had to get the truck back home. Neither one of us was anxious to take that task but Gary said he would drive the truck and I would drive Gary's car. Gary later said it was the worst trip of his life. I don't remember much about that drive except it was the longest trip I had ever taken. It took me through nineteen years of memories and a future that had ended.

I had written in my journal a couple of days before this, *". . . constantly knowing he is in the best hands possible—no matter what. God is in control."* The next entry is, Friday, June 5—*"The battle ends—the war continues. Death—where is your sting?; our victory is in the Lord Jesus Christ."* Then a quote from Larry Crabb's book, *Shattered Dreams: "The journey to joy takes us through shattered dreams, an opportunity to be embraced."*

I don't wish to minimize other causes of death and the pain and suffering they bring, but suicide is different. I can see and accept God's hand in other causes of death because the circumstances are out of my control. I grieved tremendously when my dad died. I was angry at God because He took him too early, at least in my time frame. But I had no control over his cancer and thus accepted it as God's will. But because suicide is caused by volition, it brings a lot of baggage of blame and guilt to the survivors. *Where did we go wrong? What should we have done differently? We should have seen it coming and prevented it. Somehow we could have made a difference. It didn't have to end this way.* When Scott died, all these feelings went through my head. I thought of all the ways God could have intervened to stop this tragedy, right up until that final moment. However, I realized He allowed Scott to take his life even though it probably wasn't His ultimate plan for him. God had given him so much talent that I'm sure He had more in store for him.

I remembered seeing Tony Dungy, the Indianapolis Colts' coach, on TV before Scott died. It was shortly after Dungy's son had committed suicide. I watched him on the sidelines, coaching as usual. I kept thinking, *How does he do it? How does he carry on? What's he thinking? Could he have done something to keep his son alive? Does he think he was a good father? How would I react if I were in his shoes?* Now that I was in his shoes, I didn't know if he got answers to his questions, but my answers did not come quickly or easily, especially the big question, "Why?" Now my tears were of questions, grief, disappointment in me . . . and in God. *My God, it wasn't supposed to turn out this way! We waited so long to have this only son; surely, there was a purpose in that. What glory is there now? There is only a wrenching heartache and the emptiness of hope not fulfilled.*

Chapter 17

JUNE 6

*Let the morning bring me word of your
unfailing love, for I have put my trust in you.
Show me the way I should go,
for to you I lift up my soul.
Psalm 143:8*

AS I WOKE up on June 6, 2009, heard the birds singing, and saw the sun shining, the words of a song kept running through my head. It questions why things are going on as they always had, the birds singing, the sun shining, my heart still beating, when clearly things are no longer the same because of lost love.

My world had ended. So why *did* everything go on the way it always had? The sun *was* still shining, the birds *were* still singing, and my heart kept beating even though it had been shattered in a million pieces. Didn't they know they shouldn't be doing these things? It was the end of the world! It all ended when Scott said good-bye.

I tried to put down the thoughts in my journal.

"So few words as my head reels and my heart tears apart. He mentioned suicide several times—but I remember thinking, What would I do if he really did it? Of course, my mind raced ahead to that conclusion and I didn't like it. I only wanted to think about deliverance. God, you rescued Isaac from the altar. His father was going to kill him and you provided another way, a ram was in the thicket. Where was my ram? I had so much hope that God would restore us; that we would be a family again. But I have to trust that God, even though I can't see it, is in control. Scott is joyful in the arms of Jesus. He has all the answers and someday I will, too. I have to trust that He will make something good from this, that Scott's life will not have been in vain."

My world had changed and I wanted everybody to know and feel my pain—but they didn't. I wasn't sure what my world would be like from then on. I didn't want to face that world. As I lay in bed, I tried my best to process all that had happened. I realized I needed to face my new reality. I, along with Scott, had just become a statistic. We were both victims of a teen suicide, the second leading cause of death among teenagers. I made it as far as putting one foot on the floor before I turned back to my bed and began sobbing. *Is this what it's going to be like?* I thought, *breaking down with every thought of him?* My eyes were sore from all the crying the night before. Nagging thoughts would not leave me alone—thoughts of Scott and what he had been going through, of prayers not answered, of what could have been, but mostly guilt. As I would later come to experience, guilt would be my constant companion and nemesis.

I gained my composure, got up, and went into the living room. Gary came in from the bedroom and joined me after a few minutes. We hugged again as we tried to smile, trying our best to be strong for each other. The conversation Gary and Scott had at their last meeting came to my mind. I'm sure that hug and those wonderful words of affirming love will forever be in Gary's memory.

"I guess we need to let everyone know," I said softly, not wanting to break the deafening silence between us.

"I guess so. I'll make a few phone calls."

"I need to call Susan and let her know she needs to chair the meeting I was supposed to this afternoon. After that, I'll send out some emails."

As we broke off from each other and he picked up the phone, I could hear his voice crack as he made his calls. I approached the computer. *What would I say? How much should I tell?* I couldn't get my thoughts collected. I put my head down and cried again, this time asking God's wisdom for this simple task. Not long after, responses to the emails started pouring in. It was a comfort to know so many were praying for us and keeping us in their thoughts. But now my thoughts had to be turned toward the many details that were to come.

Later that day, I wasn't expecting anyone as the doorbell rang. Opening the door, I saw a thirty-something, tall, well-built, blond man in front of me. He was dressed very casually but I did notice he was wearing a badge on his belt. He told me his name and announced he was with the police department. He handed me a small plastic bag, explaining these were the items Scott had with him at the time of his death. I almost couldn't bear to look at what I recognized as the few things Scott had in his pockets, his cell phone, his keys, his wallet. There were a few pictures of his prom night, his bank card, and his library card. His license had a recent picture with his long, sandy-blond hair curled neatly along his shoulders. His iPod was there, which held all his favorite tunes, including the Beatles and Pink Floyd. His key chain had a brightly colored picture of Pookey. My thoughts yelled out, *No, my son cannot be relegated to just these few things in this plastic bag! He was much more than these; he was a person, a very special person, not a number or statistic, or list of "personal belongings."* Releasing my gaze and memories from the bag, I looked at the man's face. His eyes were tender. I thanked him quietly and asked him to come in. After hearing some protocol about what the coroner had done the night before, I invited him to sit down on the couch. We both relaxed as we faced each other. From his warm, gracious, and gentle demeanor, I felt I could talk with him.

"I have a son that's just about to turn ten," he said smiling, "and I'm looking forward to seeing him grow up. I can't imagine losing him. I don't pretend to know what you're going through but my prayers are with you."

"Thanks, I appreciate that. My biggest comfort right now is knowing that I'm going to see him again. I know his future in heaven was secured and I know mine is as well," I told him.

I was amazed I hadn't broken down at this point, but I was relishing the thought of Scott being in the arms of Jesus.

"That would be mine as well. I am a Christian and firmly believe that that is our only hope." His eyes were sincere as he told me about his church and what he was involved in there. I, in turn, explained that Gary was the pastor of our church. It was a wonderful conversation. God had sent a kind fellow believer to do such an unpleasant task. It was just a taste of what God was going to do, showing Himself in ways I had never known. When we parted, he mentioned we needed to contact the coroner to let him know what we wanted to do with the body. I thanked him again and closed the door.

Leaning against the doorpost, my thoughts reeled. *Body! There is nobody there! Scott's gone! No more coming through this door with his laughter and "Hi, Mom." His body—an empty shell, yes, but his soul is real and in heaven with his Savior. Oh, God, get me through this!*

We decided to have his body cremated. We found a place that would take care of all the details so it was handled quite efficiently. They were very kind when they called and let us know the ashes were ready to be picked up. Gary put down the phone slowly and let me know Scott was ready to come home. We made the twenty-minute trip in silence. After meeting with the manager and taking care of the paperwork, we picked up the nicely wrapped box. She had covered it neatly with gold foil wrapping and a purple ribbon. Putting it on the backseat of the car, I said as I closed the door, with a quiver in my voice, "One last trip, Bug, buckle up."

Chapter 18

MEMORIES

I remember the days of long ago;
I meditate on all your works and consider
what your hands have done.
Psalm 143:5

So many things will spark memories of him—a
song, a smell, places we went, all triggers of times past. I was
in the kitchen, doing the dishes one morning the following
October. As I looked out the window I saw all those needles
from the huge pine tree close to the house. As I looked at the
needles steadily making a massive layer around this tree my
mind wandered back to previous fall days when Scott was in
elementary school.

"Scott, your dad asked you to rake up those pine needles.
Would you please get out there and do it?" He grabbed his
jacket and headed out the door toward Joel's house.

"I'm going over to Joel's to see if he wants to help me. That OK?" he hollered as the door slammed behind him.

"Sure," I muttered to myself. "Whatever works, I guess," returning to my chore at hand.

Moments later he returned with Joel in tow. They embarked on the task and I had to admit having the two engaged in the job kept the complaining and whining to a minimum. Our yard is large, as city lots go, with several leafy trees that make lots of leaves. Not only are there needles from the pine tree but leaves to rake as well. A cherry tree on the back corner rarely puts out cherries but sheds leaves like crazy. There are two clotheslines attached to this tree and the little apple tree about thirty feet directly across. That one puts out apples, inedible due to bugs and worms. Since we don't pick them, they just fall and make a gooey mess. Not many leaves, though. Directly across from the cherry tree, down the length of the yard almost one hundred feet is the plum tree. That one is my nemesis. Again, no fruit but it puts out horrible, spiky shoots in the grass and lots of little leaves. Following the line down that side of the yard is the birch tree. It puts out tiny little leaves that are frustrating for anybody to rake. The middle of the yard is open and grassy but little of it is without some sort of leaf, especially after a bit of wind.

As Scott and Joel started the chore, it was fun. They chattered about friends and school, and told jokes, while Joel complained about little brothers. The boys made piles of leaves and then strewed them about since the temptation was too great to resist jumping into them. However, as they found out very quickly, doing a job twice is not so much fun. As the hour wore on the chatter slowed and complaining picked up. "How long do we have to do this? I'm getting tired," Joel asked, leaning on his rake. As a lad in grade school, his attention span for lengthy jobs was quite short.

"My dad said we had to get the needles up," Scott moaned. "We have to bag 'em up, too."

"Oh, heck, we'll be here all day. I want to do something else." Joel kicked the pile of leaves.

"We'll just get these up and leave the rest. They'll be here when we get back," Scott reasoned, slowly pulling his rake around the pile.

The piles were left as the boys half-heartedly put some needles and leaves in a few bags and then made a mad dash out the yard. Later I got on his case and the job got done, under much duress. It was an ongoing struggle during the fall to keep up with the yard but there were also times when Scott and I did it together. Those were good times. I think about them often, especially when I look out the window at the job I now do on my own.

My mind always hears his voice as we talked while we raked, piled, and gathered leaves and needles.

Memories, like leaves, keep coming back. In the springtime, leaves are wonderful to look at. I love all the green tones of the different trees in our yard. Those leaves are like the good memories; the ones I like to remember. When I think about Scott playing as a young boy with Joel and his friends, those memories can be precious. But then, the winter comes and the leaves turn ugly and fall. I don't like to deal with the mess they leave on the ground. The weather is cold and wet, making the job even more unpleasant. Every time I pull the rake through leaves it's like raking my heart, picking up those bad memories and especially the guilt. Guilt piles up those bad memories and tells me how I could have been a better mother—I could have done more with him, I was too "hovering," controlling—and the list goes on. The talks we had were soul searching and I relish them. But then I think of how I should have done more to direct him, or I should have been aware of what he was doing and asked more questions. I should have . . . and the doubts continue, allowing the guilt to once more take over.

Of course, as he got more deeply involved in his transition, the big doubt had been "Did we do enough?" and the corresponding doubt, "Did we do the right thing?" At times, the guilt felt like one big pile of wet, ugly, sticky leaves, trying to smother me.

When I feel myself falling prey to this overwhelming guilt, God starts to gently pour out His Spirit. He lovingly directs my mind toward His word, which is the salve my soul needs to recover. The first verse He reminds me of is 1 John 1:9, "If we confess our sins, He is faithful and just to forgive our sins and to cleanse us from all unrighteousness." I used this verse right after Scott died. I immediately went before my Father and confessed any sins that I knew of that might have contributed to his death. I know He has forgiven me and, better yet, has forgotten them. Then the verse from Philippians 3:13, comes to mind; " . . . Forgetting those things that lie behind and reaching forward to what lies ahead." Realizing any wrongdoing already has been wiped out, I move past that. It's a freeing moment, knowing that God does not hold anything against me. So why should I dwell on sins that are no longer an issue? I can't do anything to change the past so I must accept what has happened and move on to the moment I'm in. I had to keep reminding myself so much was out of my control.

There's a scene from the movie *The Lion King* that depicts this concept vividly. Simba, next in line to be king, is depressed, thinking about his father who has recently been killed. He feels unworthy and unable to take over that position which he should assume. Rafiki, his father's advisor, encourages Simba to come and take his rightful place. After Simba voices his doubts and discouragement, Rafiki takes matters into his own hands. He shows Simba a reflection of himself in the water. Simba's father speaks to him through this reflection.

"You've forgotten who you are. Take your rightful place and be who you are. Remember who you are. You are more than what you've become."

Simba looks away, contemplating his father's words.

Rafiki approaches, "Change is good."

Simba responds, " . . . but not so easy. I'll have to face the past."

Immediately, Rafiki hits him over the head with his stick.

"Ow! What'd you do that for?"

"It doesn't matter—it's in the past!"

"Yeah, but it still hurts."

"Oh, yes, the past can hurt. But the way I look at it you can either run from it or learn from it," whereupon, Rafiki swings his stick again. But this time Simba ducks.

Rafiki smiles. "You see?"

I have thought about that many times in many ways. First, it reminds me who I am—a child of the King, One who loves me very much. As a loving Father, He continues to teach me what He knows is best for me. When the guilt comes pouring in, I recall the past. Sure it hurts. Can I change it? No! So I can either run from it, or let it eat me up, or put it behind me and let God teach me through it. Through all those years, I did what I thought I needed to do and what I thought was best. Did I make mistakes? Sure I did. Can I change what I did? Can I change what *anybody* did? Of course not. I know God has forgiven me of any wrongdoing so I move on to put in place what He is teaching me now. But those events have left scars on my heart, just like the hit Rafiki gave Simba left a scar on his head.

Scars are reminders of past injuries or events, some good and some bad. I look at the scars on my knees reminding me of my replacement surgeries. I remember the pain before I had them done. Now, I have pain-free movement and am able to resume the activities I love. It causes me to be thankful for the wonderful technology of medicine that allows me to do that. However, after surgery, the physical therapist had to remind me to work on my scar. I had to massage it regularly to allow it to be pliable with the surrounding skin. If I didn't, it would become tight and not allow the knee to move as it should. I was faithful to do that and I reaped the benefits. The scar on my heart is not so easily fixed. It still has tender spots that aren't quite healed. I use God's word to massage it regularly to allow it to be pliable for what He wants to do in my life.

Scars can be tender for a long time and easily torn open. In one sense, I'm thankful for those scars. God uses those rips on the scars of my heart to do several things in my life. As the memories cut on those sensitive scars He reminds me of what He has done in the past, bringing me through the fire of testing. He reminds me of His faithfulness to His word. I often go to Psalm 42:5, "Why are you in despair, O my soul? And why have you become disturbed within me? Hope in God, for I shall again praise Him for the help of His presence." Despair? Disturbed? Oh, for sure, I am, even yet. But the last lines are the comfort I have " . . . I shall again praise Him for the help of His presence."

I don't like facing the past since it brings up feelings of guilt and anger. But God is showing me how looking at those scars in the light of His word can be good and life changing. His presence has become more real. I have realized He truly is the only hope I have. In one of my moments of despair shortly after Scott died, I was reading some passages in Philippians and it was like God hit *me* over the head. He made me aware that I needed to literally take God at His word and believe every word of every promise He has written.

When we eat we put food in our mouth and chew it. But it doesn't become a part of us, or do us any good, until we actually *swallow* it. That's what I had been doing with God's word. I was chewing on His promises, taking them out, reciting them, and putting them back for more chewing—but never swallowing! Finally, Psalm 34:8 came alive, "Taste and see that the Lord is good." I actually *swallowed* and *tasted* all those promises He had given me. I believed with all my heart, soul, and mind that He could and would do everything He promised. I had to. He was my only lifeline to keep me out of the mire of despair, hopelessness, guilt, and anger. I had found a new trust in God that I had not experienced before.

I didn't fully realize how much I had wanted my own way and to remain in control. I was trusting in myself to provide plans, thinking I had everything to make sure those plans worked out. I even had escape plans in case those I planned didn't come through. I had lulled myself into thinking, *Surely, this is what God would want me to do—everything seems reasonable. Obviously, this is God's will.*

I was doing the same thing to God that I was accusing Scott of doing to us—demanding God prove His love by what He does. I expected Him to bless my plans. I was asking God *after the fact* instead of laying myself on the altar of His will. I wanted Him to bless my plans and show Himself through the performance of those plans. Oh, I told everybody, including myself, that I was trusting God fully. In reality, I was holding back. It was like I was standing on the edge of the pool as God called me to jump into His waiting arms. I realized I was waiting for Him to come and lift me up off the edge of the pool instead of trusting Him to catch me as I jumped into His arms. I could not truly say, *Whatever Lord, Your will be done.* But now He had brought me through my worst-case scenario. My greatest "what if" had happened. It wasn't my plan. It wasn't in any of my escape plans; it was my greatest nightmare! He had shown me the futility of my plans and His overriding sovereignty.

Chapter 19

PARENTING

And, fathers, do not provoke
your children to anger;
but bring them up in the discipline
and instruction of the Lord.
Ephesians 6:4 (NASB)

"In a minute, Sweetie, Grandma's busy right now," my friend said, stooping down to talk calmly with her granddaughter.

Please, take time with her, I thought. I don't mind. You will have so little time with her. Savor those moments, because I will never have even one.

I tried to keep my self-pity at bay. At moments like these, sitting with a friend who is a grandmother, it becomes very difficult. I try not to think of what could have been. Not to think of what was ripped away from me, of the grandchildren

I will never have, of . . . and my mind starts to reel. Pulling my thoughts back to our momentarily interrupted conversation I smile and carry on. Little do they know how big a hole has just been ripped open in my heart.

I am at the age where most of my friends have grandchildren. But God has given me peace. I can truly say, as in the Romans 12:15 passage, "Rejoice with those who rejoice." I celebrate with them as they revel in sharing the lives of these children. I smile warmly as they show pictures of the newborns in the arms of beaming parents. I marvel at the cute things that little ones are doing in the videos. I congratulate them at their accomplishments in college. Sharing that happiness with them is wonderful. Yet, even with assurance of God's peace, self-pity rears its ugly head. I need to guard my thoughts from envy, realizing I will never have these moments.

I remember how blessed I was to have my son for the nineteen years I had him. I cannot let myself sink into that hole of "woe is me" when God has done so much for me. He has taught me so much about Himself.

I jokingly say I was the world's best parent for eighteen years—until I became one. During those eighteen years that I was married and childless, I had all the answers to the problems my friends were having with their children. I could tell them all the solutions, if they would just ask. Of course, I wouldn't volunteer any of my wonderful advice as that would be too presumptuous of me, but *my* children certainly wouldn't do any of those annoying things that these parents allowed their children to do. However, deep down, as is the case with most overly confident behavior, I was scared of parenthood.

I became pregnant at thirty-nine. When I found out I was pregnant, I broke out in a cold sweat. My first thought, *Really? At age thirty-nine you're not ready?* Now, suddenly, all those things I had seen my friends go through with their children came rushing into my head, things I would now have to deal with. However, just as I was getting *somewhat* used to the idea, something happened.

Gary and I decided to take a nice vacation before parenting duties would tie us down. We headed to Hawaii. It was a great five days. We saw all the sights, we snorkeled, we did luaus, we relaxed on the beach watching awesome sunsets. We had driven from New Mexico and had flown out of Portland (after visiting family there) and wanted to start for home as soon as possible upon returning to Portland. We headed back within a short time of landing, but as we entered Utah, I started spotting. I felt OK but knew that even a little bit was not good. By the time we got to New Mexico, it definitely was not good. I called the hospital and was connected with my doctor who just happened to be there.

"Dr. Graham? This is Judy Glenney. You don't know me but I'm scheduled to see you in about a week. I'm three months along and I'm bleeding. What should I do?"

"Come in right away. I'll be here so just ask for me," he said calmly.

We arrived at the hospital and were introduced. He set up the ultrasound equipment and showed me the monitor.

"Well, I see a little body," he said as he swept the handle over my belly.

"Where's the head?" I asked as I peered sideways at the screen.

"Here's the head, and here's the back. But I don't see a beating heart. I'm so sorry."

My eyes lingered at the image on the screen. It was amazing. Even though there was no life in this little body, the miracle that this tiny being could one day be a baby that would have little legs that would run, little arms that would wave, and a face that would smile and laugh was amazing. As I looked at that little, lifeless form in my body I knew without a shadow of a doubt that I wanted a baby—trouble and all!

Putting away the machine and leaning on the rail of my bed, he just looked at me with a slight smile of resignation. "Unfortunately, all we can do is a D&C and clean out the womb."

"OK," I sighed. The tears began to come as our eyes met. I realized what was happening. There was a baby in my body and even as lifeless as it was, I loved that tiny being. But I was not going to be a mother when I left the hospital.

The doctor left the room and began preparations. Wiping the tears from my eyes, I knew God had done a work in my soul that day. God had shown me I was ready to be a parent in a very clear way. Almost a year to that date Scott was born and I joined the ranks of parenthood.

I never fully understood God's love until I held that miracle of life in my arms. I began to realize how deep God's love for His children was. My love for my child was all-consuming. Being the perfect Father, how much more does He love me. I immediately thought of the phrase in Matthew where Jesus says, if we as humans know how to give good gifts to our children, how much more will our Heavenly Father give us? I was prepared to provide everything for my child. In the same way I knew I could depend on my Heavenly Father to do that for me. Unlike my baby who couldn't communicate what he needed or wanted, my Heavenly Father always knew what I needed.

As time passed, he was able to communicate with us, thankfully. When I heard him say, "Mom," my heart leapt. Never was there a sweeter sound to my ears. Even when he was upset with me, I never tired of hearing that endearing term. I suppose that must be what my Father feels when I call Him "Abba." Just as I treasured those talks with Scott, heart-to-heart, He waits anxiously for me to come before Him, heart-to-heart. There were many occasions when I would wait for Scott to tell me about things in school or merely what he'd been doing lately. But so often he would rush out the door to play or get so wrapped up in something else that he wouldn't take the time to talk. Unfortunately, that's too often the case with me. God is just waiting for me to talk with Him and tell Him about my cares and joys. But off I go to a meeting or a forgotten errand, letting another time with Him slip by.

As Scott grew, I began to communicate my love in different ways. Some ways were gentle and loving. I would write an encouraging word on a piece of paper and put it in his lunch bag. He always enjoyed the special treat I gave him after school. When he started driving, he was thrilled when I let him use the car unexpectedly. These were all in addition to the spontaneous hugs that were frequently given, overt gestures of my love. But *his* random hugs were the most precious to me. He had the best hugs! All of these were followed with the words, "Love you, Mom." What pleasure to have that love returned in such an amazing way.

However, there were also those unfortunate times in my duties as a parent when showing love was not quite so gentle. Discipline was never easy. When I was a child and heard the expression, "This hurts me more than it hurts you," I thought, *Really? You're the one giving it, not getting it! I can't wait until I'm a parent.* Well, now I was the parent and found out how true that was. It did hurt me to discipline my child but I knew it had to be done. I took no pleasure in giving those occasional swats. Taking away privileges when I knew it would cause a backlash wasn't my biggest thrill. In no way did I look forward to any form of punishing him. But it was part of loving him, guiding him, and protecting him. It came with being a good parent.

I came to understand God does the same with me as His child. There are the wonderful times when I'm walking close to Him and I notice those little "love notes" He sends me. They come in the form of laughing together with close friends; hearing songs with wonderful words of encouragement; reading verses that leap at me from the pages of His word. All these are special moments from my Heavenly Father, just for me. I'm overtaken with joy as I am overwhelmed with what He has done for me! I can imagine He enjoys "spiritual hugs" as I surrender fully to His love. Expressing that love to others is, I'm sure, even more special to Him.

Then come those moments of discipline. Oh, how I shrink from them. He particularly uses other people to tell me when I need to change my way of thinking or acting. He uses circumstances to teach me a lesson I should have known before. Then there are the repercussions of poor choices I've made. He uses these all for the same purpose; to demonstrate His love, guidance, and protection for me.

Even though I will miss out on the next chapter of love that I looked forward to, that of being a grandparent, I am thankful I had the opportunity to get to know His love in this small way. Parenthood is just a rough estimate of what God's love is toward me. God had given me one son. In His perfect plan, He took this son. That was not my idea, certainly not in my plans whatsoever. I cannot imagine what it would be like to *willingly* give up my son, knowing the pain it causes. God had one Son. He willingly gave His Son to die a cruel death because He loved me that much. "For God so loved the world (*which includes me*) that He gave His only Son, that whosoever (*which includes me*) believes in Him should not perish but have everlasting life." (John 3:16) I can't help but think of His matchless love for me when I think of my only son. I give thanks to my Heavenly Father for the lessons of love He sends, hard though they are to understand.

Chapter 20

REMINDERS

I say to myself, "The Lord is my portion;
therefore I will wait for him.
Lamentations 3:24

Muscle memory. We hear this term most often used in sports. However, we use muscle memory in everyday life more than we realize. By definition, it is when a movement is repeated over time so that a long-term muscle memory, or pattern, is created for that task. This eventually allows the movement to be performed without conscious effort. Athletes strive to perfect their performance by practicing the same movement over and over again, hopefully, in a precise manner. This translates to the wonderful movements we see them exhibit in competition, at the Olympics. We marvel at their execution as they make those complicated moves look effortless. What we haven't seen are the thousands of repetitions they did before they ever got to that point. But do we think about how to ride a bicycle? Or work on a keyboard? Or walk? We have performed those tasks so many times we just do them without thinking. It's the same with our minds. We need to train our "spiritual muscles" to respond automatically to those tests God gives us. We can only do that by having His word in our souls. Only by hearing it countless times can we do that.

Repetition is the key to remembering anything. We need to hear things many times before we learn. Over and over in scripture, God says "Remind them of these things," or "Bring this to their remembrance." Clearly, we need to have our memories jogged about what God has said or done for us before it sticks in our minds. I know I have a very short memory when it comes to learning lessons, especially those trust lessons. As a teacher, I am fully aware of this reminding concept. I have a tendency to get impatient with students who seem to forget everything I've just said. At that point, God reminds me He has to do the same with me. So I patiently repeat the instructions or concept, hopefully more clearly. I do this by emphasizing important words, saying it several different ways, or demonstration—anything that would help them comprehend it.

God once brought this to my attention in a vivid fashion. It was our anniversary and I wanted to make it special. I had made arrangements for a dinner cruise. Checking out all the details, I thought I had it all under control. I knew the time we needed to board and looked up the directions on Google Maps. I wasn't all that familiar with where the dock was, but I figured I could find it. I took extra time getting dressed, putting on a special outfit. I truly wanted to make it a night to remember. We left in plenty of time to be there early. Gary asked if I knew where we were going. Telling him I had a pretty good idea, I laid the directions beside me as I got in the driver's seat. We took off, looking forward to a wonderful date. As I drove around the area where I thought the exit was, I discovered it wasn't where I thought it was. We started to go farther down the road. Realizing I was now away from any point of water, I got antsy. Gary kept questioning. I was way out of my element and had no idea where I was. Time was getting dangerously short. I decided to turn around and head back, thinking I had missed some indicators for the dock along the way. Nothing was looking like it would get us to the river. I became frustrated and started to panic. It was now boarding time. It became clear we were not going to make this cruise.

I darted around corners, backed around streets, and took undue chances to get there. Gary finally said, "Calm down. It's OK. We'll go another time."

"No, it's not! They won't honor our tickets any other time!" I began to cry as my night to remember was turning into anything but special.

"So what? It's not worth the aggravation you're putting yourself through."

With that, I pulled over and Gary got in the driver's seat and drove home. When we reached the house, he reminded me who's in control and that it was just a detail of life.

"But I wanted this night to be special and it turned out all wrong," I said sadly, putting my head on his shoulder.

Hugging me tightly, he just whispered, "Happy anniversary, anyway."

As it turned out, I called the cruise line the next day and they said they would honor our reservations the next weekend with no problem. It boarded from a different location, much easier to find. We had a wonderful anniversary dinner. We talked with people that I'm sure God had intended for us to meet on that special night. His divine appointment. I was humbled again, thinking I had the best plan when He made it very clear His plan always has the best outcome.

Although He has taken me through many situations, in which I had to realize (always in hindsight) that I should trust His leading, this time He had really brought the lesson home. I have recalled this several times since. When I start to panic in a situation and things aren't going my way, He brings to my mind, "Remember the boat." I know it's working out for the best, even though at the time things seem to be unraveling. God really does know what He's doing. He has to continually drive home the point that in *all* things I need to let go, relax, and know that He is God. Let Him have the reins, as I know He is in control.

Those moments of epiphany can come at odd times. I was on the mountain. It was a gorgeous day for skiing—blue sky, no wind, great snow, just about perfect. I was heading up the slopes on the chairlift, admiring the view, or so I thought. As I looked around I realized I really *wasn't* admiring the view. My thoughts were far from the beautiful mountain looming in front of me or the feel of the sun on my face. My thoughts were racing toward the drive home, what I needed to do to prepare for dinner, and the numerous things I had on my "to do" list. All of a sudden it hit me as I was looking at the bright sunlight.

You're up here on a fantastic day that God has given you to enjoy and where is your head? This is the moment He's given you to enjoy; this is where He wants you to be right now, in this moment.

I find myself running way ahead of where I should be. If I am truly walking with Him moment by moment, then each moment is His to do with as He sees fit. He has placed me at that place, at that time, for a purpose.

Anthony Bloom writes about "stopping time" in his book, *Beginning to Pray.* He said that stopping time transformed his life with God. He focused on the present, knowing the past is already gone and the future is, in fact, irrelevant because we don't know if it will even take place. *Now,* this fleeting moment, is in fact our intersection of eternity with time.

That time on the mountain was a time for me to enjoy the ability He's given me to relish His wonders in a physical way. Other moments may not be so enjoyable. However, they are still His moments He's given me for a purpose. If I am faithful to do what He has called me to do at every moment, the results will always be as He intended. He will continue to review with me the trust lessons. As the perfect Teacher, He will find new and different ways to remind me of the concept. *Lord, make me a willing student that I may trust you completely.*

Chapter 21

TRUSTING

Trust in the Lord with all your heart,
And do not lean on your own understanding.
Proverbs 3:5

"You've got to keep the bar closer. Pull it to the stick—more speed! You can do this, *trust me.*" Gary was in his coaching role. These were cues and instructions, all meant for the best possible results. *Trust me?* I thought, *I have no choice. You know this sport!*

After Gary and I met in that weight room, where he introduced me to weightlifting, I recognized him as one who knew the sport and he recognized in me one who *wanted* to know the sport. He immediately became my coach after we married. Living with your coach, twenty-four seven, normally does not work out for the best. However, in our case it worked out great, usually. We got to know each other, that's for sure. Because this was a new endeavor for me, I had to learn to trust him in that capacity. He had competed for many years and had won many competitions, so he proved himself capable of coaching me. I had visions of being a champion and I knew he could help me get there.

In my first few meets I was, naturally, quite nervous. Was I going to be prepared? Was I going to be ready when my name was called to lift on the platform? Would I be at the right bodyweight? All these questions were going through my head since I wasn't familiar with the process of competition. Gary tried to prepare me by telling me what was going to happen. However, when I got to the meet nerves took over and I forgot much of what he told me. He then stepped in and told me he had everything under control, saying calmly, "Trust me." He would lead me through everything. I just had to concentrate on my lifting.

The "everything" he was referring to were the details that go on behind the scenes. Much strategy is involved within the competition. Each lifter has three attempts in both the snatch and clean-and-jerk lifts to attain the greatest weight lifted. The coach must be aware of each lifter's attempts in order to select the weight needed for his lifter to place as high as possible. At least one attempt in each category must be made to be eligible for a place in the competition. One very important point: the weight on the bar never reduces. All the lifters declare the weight they want for their first attempt as they weigh in. This is usually a weight he or she knows can be made easily, to assure getting that one success. The lifter with the lowest announced starting weight begins the competition. If the lifter is successful at that weight, the bar is loaded to the next highest weight a lifter has requested. If a lifter fails his attempt, the option is to repeat the weight or go up in weight. Meanwhile, the lifters are in the back area warming up for their attempts. The coach has to be on top of several things at once. He has to watch the weight on the bar, observe how many attempts are being made before his lifter is called, and get the lifter adequately warmed up. Many shifts in attempts can happen at the last minute so he has to watch constantly.

All I had to do was allow him to direct me. He told me when to warm up. He kept me apprised of when I was to be on the platform to lift. Being nervous and anxious, I wanted to speed things up. That was the toughest part for me—waiting patiently for my turn. Gary had to constantly tell me to relax and save my energy. When my turn finally came to lift, he sent me out with his last words of encouragement, "Just do what you know to do." Learning the technique of the snatch and clean and jerk takes many tedious hours of practice. He knew I was ready because he had tested my technique in the gym. Now came the "big test"—competition. He reminded me that he had gotten me ready. I simply had to do what we had practiced.

This is much like my walk with God. He is the ultimate coach. I have to trust him fully. The hours of Bible study and the little tests He puts me through can be arduous, just like all those hours in the gym. But I know the preparation is necessary if I'm going to pass the test of the competition. The "competition" we face in life are those major tests He gives us. First of all, He knows us and knows when we're ready. Gary didn't put me in my first meet until he felt I was competent in the technique. 1 Corinthians 10:13 tells us that God doesn't give us anything in our lives until He feels we're ready to handle it, under His control. Then, He wants us to trust Him fully to get us through the test. He guides us through it, gently reminding us of verses He has taught us, the past trials He has brought us through, and the doctrines we learned that we can now apply.

I have gone to some meets without Gary. They didn't work out well. One competition was particularly important since it was the first Masters World Championship. I wanted to do especially well because I was the "leading lady" in the weight-lifting movement for women. Gary was not able to be with me since he needed to be home with Scott. I asked a friend, whom I knew coached several elite lifters, to watch my attempts and get me warmed up. He was more than happy to oblige since he had no lifters in the competition. I counted my own attempts until my first lift. I had an idea about when I would be starting but counted on him to watch for changes. I was in the back, taking my time warming up.

"You've got about ten attempts. You're fine," Bob told me as he peeked his head in the warm-up area. Feeling he had things under control, I set my mind on my warm-up strategy. I wanted this to be a record-setting meet.

I slowed down so as not to waste energy. Knowing that I had a tendency to take too many warm ups, I paced myself. I wanted to take three more lifts with lighter weights, to get my head into lifting the heavier weight on the platform for my first attempt. Sitting still, I mentally went through my technique. I thought about all those things Gary had told me. *Speed! Finish your pull! Get your first lift in, make it easy, and go from there.* I smiled as I heard his voice in my head. I tried not to look down the road to what I wanted to make; I needed to focus on one lift at a time. I looked at the weight. Thinking all was going smoothly, I approached. All of a sudden, I heard my name being called. I was on deck! I was to be the next lifter! It was hard to control the panic that immediately came over me.

Bob was nowhere to be found. I started yanking off my sweatpants as I broke out in a cold sweat. I was totally unprepared! The next thing I know, in comes Bob.

"Hey, you're up. You've got one minute to get to the platform."

I threw my sweats on the floor and darted out.

"You were supposed to watch my attempts!" I glared at him as I approached the platform.

"I thought you had them under control," he responded casually.

I bolted out to the platform, at which point I had mere seconds to lift the weight before it would be counted as a missed attempt. My mind was every place but on the weight. Ripping the bar off the floor, I failed miserably.

"Do you want to repeat with that weight?" Bob had the audacity to ask.

"Yes," I told him as I tried to compose myself. Grabbing my sweats off the floor, I thought, *Thanks for nothing. I was coming in this meet in great shape, hoping to make all my attempts. A wasted effort. But gather yourself; put it behind you, make the next ones and go on.*

I went back to prepare for my second attempt. I heard him give me some "encouragement" as I walked back to the warm-up room.

"Really pull it from the floor. Get it up high," he said in a low voice. I don't know if he did or didn't want me to hear. But I did hear and it was very distracting.

I thought, *Don't say anything if you don't know what I need to hear, and that certainly isn't what I need to hear.*

Now he came over to the platform where I was lifting. "What weight do you want on the bar?" he asked as he bent over the weights in anticipation of putting them on the bar.

"That's OK, I'll get it," I replied, trying now to just be civil. I knew I was coming up shortly so I just sat down and waited a few minutes. I was up. Heading out to the platform I was totally out of the groove, so, unfortunately, I missed that one as well.

"Thanks, Bob, I think I can take it from here," I told him, as I walked off the platform, trying to keep my emotions in check. I had to get him out of my periphery if I was going to salvage anything from this competition. I went on to make the third attempt and make enough on my clean and jerks to win the championship. But the result was far from my expectations and my capability. I had become too distracted to focus on my lifting.

We tend to do things on our own when the crisis hits. We get so wrapped up in the details. We worry about everything around us. Therefore, we can't do what we need to be doing, namely, trusting our "training." When we lean on other people, they usually lead us in the wrong direction, thereby producing ill consequences.

That's not to say I always did great with Gary there. In some cases, I let nerves get the better of me. I got my eyes on my competitors or I let the weight itself overcome me by doubting my abilities. After each meet we would go through what happened, especially if I did poorly. He could evaluate much better than I because he had the whole picture, looking at everything that was going on. I only knew what it *felt* like. Back in the gym we would train harder on those weak areas. This shows another important point. Gary, as with all my coaches, was not accountable to me where my training was concerned. He didn't have to tell me why he was doing certain things in my workouts. He expected me to trust him. I knew that what he was doing was best for me. He was giving me what I needed to be able to do my best when it counted, thereby producing the best possible outcome. Working over those weak points wasn't easy but it was necessary.

The one thing that God impressed upon me during those first months after Scott's death was to trust God's character. I had learned, and even taught, this doctrine in many ways through the years. When the crisis hit, that character was the one thing God said to trust. He seemed to say, "You know this, trust Me now—trust Who and What I am."

These are the truths He brought to my attention: His sovereignty—He is in complete control; His omniscience—He knows everything about the situation, even the smallest details; He knows me and loves me, therefore, He won't do anything that isn't the best for me; His omnipresence—He will be with me every step of the way. I once heard a speaker say, "You will not understand God by what He does, but rather by Who He is, by His character." I have found that so true. What more could I ask for in the perfect Coach! I will never understand completely why He does certain things in my life. But I certainly have learned to trust Him more completely through His testing. Jerry Bridges, in his book, *Trusting God, Even When Life Hurts*, sums it up.

"There is no question that adversity is difficult. It usually takes us by surprise and seems to strike where we are most vulnerable. To us it often appears completely senseless and irrational, but to God none of it is either senseless or irrational. He has a purpose in every pain He brings or allows in our lives. We can be sure that in some way He intends it for our profit and His glory." I can only say, "Amen."

Chapter 22

LESSONS IN PRAYER

I know not by what methods rare,
But this I know—God answers prayer.
I know not if the blessings sought
Will come in just the way I thought;
But I leave my prayers to Him alone,
Whose will is wiser than my own.

These words by Eliza Hickok though pleasing to the ear, are a powerful lesson about prayer. I wrestled with each idea she portrays in this lovely poem. The year previous to Scott's death I struggled, questioning whether my prayers even mattered. During the ensuing years after Scott's death God turned my thinking around 180 degrees.

If I look at each line separately, I find two distinct perspectives; one before Scott died and a second after his death. God reshaped my view not only about prayer but about my relationship with Him as well. He has truly become my "Abba," my Heavenly Father.

"I know not by what methods rare."

God created us with a finite mind. We are not omniscient as He is. This makes us trust Him and have faith in *His* omniscience. During the last two years of Scott's life, did I believe He knew all we were going through? I think so, but my thought was, *Why doesn't He do something about it?* I definitely couldn't see beyond my circumstances, and my thinking and emotions reflected that. I was stuck in my immediate situation. My finite mind held me captive to what I could perceive as immediate possibilities. My pain was real, so I looked for tangible solutions. My prayers were directed to that logical end, getting rid of the pain.

I gave God many suggestions about how He could take care of the problem. The answers I looked for were within those boundaries, and I expected God to deliver in that realm. I groped for counselors, for medications, for doctors, anything I could think of that would make the pain go away immediately, both for Scott and for us. None of these worked; in fact, difficulties started to escalate. As they did, I felt the doors of heaven close and God turn a deaf ear to my prayers. I pleaded, I yelled, I cried, I did all I could to get God's attention. Many were the nights I would cry myself to sleep in exasperation, only to awaken to another day of frustration. I just knew He had to answer my prayer and in the way I determined.

I didn't want to think of other ways God would answer my fervent pleading with Him. I didn't want to accept any alternative to my plan. He *had* to answer my prayer *this* way! Thinking outside my little box was not possible. He put me outside that box in showing me His amazing love.

I have come to realize God's love is shown in "His methods rare." Pain is part of love. To many of us that is an oxymoron. However, C.S. Lewis put it well when he said, "God whispers in our pleasures . . . and shouts in our pain." Only because God loves us so much does He give us the opportunity to trust Him more. He accepts us the way we are but loves us too much to leave us that way. Changing us to draw us closer to Him is His desire. He does that through His omniscience, knowing exactly what we need to accomplish that. I finally heard His shouts.

God in His perfect wisdom knew what Scott could bear. I had to trust that God loved him as much as He loved me and thought it best to allow him to come home. Once again I had to relinquish my imperfect mother's love into the perfect Father's care.

I know Scott is free from pain and that gives me comfort. Because of that I'm not questioning God as I did. That's what is rare about His ways; they are beyond our scope. But thanks be to God for His endless love, regardless of what I do. My part is to trust and submit to His methods no matter what, and even if I don't understand.

The suffering has done me good. Would I have chosen it this way? No, certainly not. Pain is pain and it hurts. But I know He has produced from it the good that He promised He would. He has spoken very clearly in Psalm 46:10, "be still, and *know that I am God.*"

"But this I know—God answers prayer."

I questioned that to my very core. God *didn't* answer my prayer! Things got worse! There were more arguments. There was also deafening silence. Scott's lying and deceit intensified.

I prayed for wisdom regarding these issues. But nothing was resolved and the discussions became more heated. I heard no startling wisdom coming out of my mouth that would change anything. Where were the answers?

Somehow I must have missed something. Maybe I had unconfessed sin in my life. Maybe I had the wrong motive. Maybe I had done something wrong. Maybe I hadn't obeyed Him in what He wanted me to do. Maybe it was . . . my mind wandered to all sorts of places. All of those thoughts were blaming myself. The biggest reason, I deduced, must have been my lack of faith. I kept going back to Matthew 17:20, " . . . if you have faith as a mustard seed, you shall say to this mountain, 'Move from here to there,' and it shall move; and nothing shall be impossible to you." I tried my hardest to "muster" up that kind of faith, not knowing for sure what kind I needed or how much. But according to that scripture, I didn't need much.

Philip Yancey wrote, "The kind of faith God values seems to develop best when everything fuzzes over, when God stays silent, when the fog rolls in." The fog certainly did roll in during those last months. It truly did seem God was not listening to my fervent prayers. I concluded God did not answer my prayer. I thought my requests were right and true, in line with God's will. Because God did not answer according to my plan, I wrongly assumed God was not listening and answering my prayer. Thus the fog was engulfing me. However, God lifted that fog and began to reveal to me how He really does hear and answer every prayer.

When I didn't get the expected answer, I questioned the very notion of prayer. Why pray if God doesn't listen? Besides, His prayer conditions sounded confusing. The more I looked into prayer, the more I was perplexed. Thoughts whirled in my head. *He says He will give us anything we ask for. On the other hand we have to ask according to His will. How do I know what His will is? How do I know I will get what I ask for if I don't know that I'm asking according to His will? He also says we have to have the right motive. How do know I have the right motive? If I doubt I may not get an answer. Doubts? With all those conditions about prayer going on I don't have doubts? No wonder I don't get answers!* Then I started to peek through the fog.

I went to the Bible. I wanted to see the response of others who had not had prayers answered.

The first response reveals what must have been Jesus' most anxious and grievous moments in His humanity. "And He went a little beyond them, and fell to the ground, and began to pray that if it were possible, the hour might pass Him by. And He was saying, "Abba! Father! All things are possible for Thee; remove this cup from Me; yet not what I will, but what Thou will." (Mark 14:35,36) That short prayer told me a lot about prayer. Jesus, God's Son, poured out His heart to His Father. Deity aside, He knew what to expect just from His humanity.

From His human aspect, He pled with His Father to allow Him not to go through the pain He knew was coming. But He submitted to God the Father and His will. Thankfully, He knew the plan for His life would mean much more for so many that He would sacrifice the life He had to give.

A second response I saw was the apostle Paul. He pleaded with God to take his infirmity (whatever it was) from him. I certainly identified with this, as many others have. We pray many times for the deliverance of something we don't like in our life. Paul only asked three times. I didn't stop at three—my petition was continuous! But the answer was the same; no. Did Paul have unconfessed sin in his life? I doubt it.

I had little trouble believing God could deliver us but my doubt was whether He *would* do it. Because I knew God is omnipotent I knew He could do anything. He could turn Scott around; He could restore our family; He could make everything brand new again. But my doubt was in His will. Would He do it? It still required letting go and accepting His will, even if it meant not getting my requested answer. I eventually came around to agree with God's answer to Paul, "My grace is sufficient for you, for *My* power is perfected in weakness." (2 Corinthians 12:9) I had to accept for myself what Jesus said, "Not my will, but Thine be done."

Things were going pretty well until all this turmoil broke loose in my life. I had a healthy, happy family, difficulties with money were getting better, and life in general was going smoothly. But inside my soul, I knew there was something missing. I knew plenty of Bible verses and principles. But I wasn't experiencing the deep, real relationship with God that

I knew I could have. I heard people talk so freely about their "friendship" with God. I wanted what they had but didn't know how to get it. I finally realized what I was missing stemmed from not fully trusting Him—holding on to what little control I had. So when all the plans I had were exhausted, I was afraid of what God was going to do. I was fearful He was going to take me where I didn't want to go, physically and spiritually. Of course, He did.

Yancey addresses this. He says that we need to turn our thoughts, not to the *why* but to *what* I can learn from this, now that it has happened. He says that the response is what is important and what is learned from the experience. The focus is thus on the productive value of suffering, the good that it can produce in my life, perseverance, patience, character, hope. This is the question I now had to ask: What is God producing now that He has put this in my life?

But there's another option, says Jerry Sittser in his book, *When God Doesn't Answer Your Prayers*. "It could be that there is no such thing as unanswered prayer. What we interpret as 'no' might really be 'not in that way' or 'not yet.' In other words, the waiting itself might be necessary, creative, and useful, like watching a forest gradually recover from a devastating fire until it becomes more beautiful than before."

After Scott's death, God brought to me a verse I memorized years ago: "Call unto me and I will answer and show you great and mighty things which you do not know." (Jeremiah 33:3) He brought that phrase "*I will answer*" continually to my thoughts. Indeed, He *did* answer my prayer. He just didn't do it in my expected way. God had to show me that I had fallen into a lot of misconceptions about prayer and my relationship with Him. "No" is a bona fide answer. However, most times we don't want to accept it. As parents, we don't always give our children what they want. When they ask for an explanation, we simply say, "Because I said so." We expect them to trust us, that we have good motives for denying them the request.

"I know not if the blessings sought, Will come in just the way I thought"

I had been taught a lot about prayer. But the way I thought, and expected, my answer to come was not a result of that teaching. Rather, it was what I wanted to *believe* about prayer. I recalled verses about prayer, "I will do whatever you ask in my name, so that the Father may be glorified in the Son. You may ask me for anything in my name, and I will do it." (John 14:13-14); "If you remain in me and my words remain in you, ask whatever you wish, and it will be done for you." (John 15:7) I was more concerned about the expected outcome than about being open to other answers He might give.

I did trust Him on a superficial level, giving mere assent to trust rather than fully surrendering to Him. I didn't want to surrender fully because I could not comprehend how I would ever handle things getting worse. I was still holding on desperately to *my plan*. I clung to the thought that God would certainly turn Scott around and see us all through this storm with a happy ending.

As parents, we use various ways to help our children learn about God. One way we taught Scott Bible verses and principles was through CDs. On these CDs, the speaker teaches a group of young children verses through songs then teaches biblical values using those verses and Bible stories.

I often think about those CDs and Scott. It happened when he was about five years old. Apparently, he had not been listening very well in Sunday School and his teacher talked with him after class. He was in the hallway with her and we just happened to be in earshot of the conversation.

"Scotty, you weren't behaving very nicely in class today," the teacher said as she sternly looked into his eyes. Scott had nothing to say as he looked back at her, obviously not wanting to be engaged in this discussion as he fidgeted.

"Do you know what obey means, Scotty?" she asked, wanting to make sure she got her point across.

Without hesitation, Scott looked at her, cocked his head to the side, shrugged and said, "I think I have a CD on that." We didn't hear if the teacher had a response since we had to turn away to cover our chuckling.

I found I was doing that very same thing with God and what He was trying to teach me. I had heard the doctrines of prayer and of God's character and had filed them away in my memory bank but never *learned* them. God was teaching me to *live* them. I just didn't expect to learn them this way.

Jerry Sittser's reflections brought it home to me again, reminding me of God's true purpose. God's greatest answer to my prayer was not in changing the circumstances. His answer was His most precious gift of God dwelling in me, helping me become more like the person He intended me to become, regardless of the circumstances. It was not the blessing I was seeking at the time but it became the greater blessing that I sought. God changed me from the inside, rather than changing things on the outside as I had desired.

Unlike Jesus, I didn't know what was in store down the road when I was praying so fervently. But like Jesus I was pleading with the Father to have it go another way because of the pain. I didn't know it would result in more pain than I had ever known before. I just knew it hurt now. I knew the doctrine of suffering and knew God had something in mind as I was going through this. Several passages about suffering illustrate this:

"Consider it all joy, my brethren, when you encounter various trials." (James 1:2)

"For I consider that the sufferings of this present time are not worthy to be compared with the glory that is to be revealed to us." (Romans 8:18)

"No temptation has overtaken you but such as is common to man; and God is faithful, who will not allow you to be tempted beyond what you are able, but with the temptation will provide the way of escape also, that you may be able to endure it." (1 Corinthians 10:13)

They seemed all so esoteric. I tried to identify with them but I couldn't see how God was going to use this suffering except by getting me out of it. Where was my "way of escape?" I tried to keep in mind there would be an end. But I still anticipated the end that I wanted. I definitely could not "count it all joy" then as the passage in James exhorts. The joy came later.

I will never forget the image of the parking lot where they found Scott's body in the truck. The sight of the coroner's van and people standing around talking in whispers will be forever embedded in my mind. It was as if a knife tore through my heart and ripped it apart. However, God gave me the comfort of knowing, without a shadow of a doubt, that Scott was with his Father in heaven. That meant he was out of pain and had all the answers. That in itself was a blessing. There was joy that our separation was only temporary and that one day I will be reunited with him. But God didn't stop there. He gave me the encouragement that if that fact were true, wasn't every promise true? Certainly!

I went back through those promises that I had so glibly read many times before and focused on what they were saying. I started to take Him literally at His word. When He says "all things work together for good," (Romans 8:28) I trusted He meant what He said. It may not have seemed like it as I grieved but maybe He would reveal something later that was for good. I looked at the promise "my God shall supply all your needs" (Philippians 4:19) differently. Before, I took that to mean all my physical needs. But I discovered I had *spiritual* needs as well. He brought to my attention how He was supplying those needs as He convicted me of my lack of trust and submission. What blessing and joy He brought in ways I never sought!

God has used struggles in my life to allow me to become the person He created me to be. The blessings I receive, and am continuing to receive, are certainly not in the ways I thought.

"But I leave my prayers to Him alone, Whose will is wiser than my own"

During those difficult months, I knew I should pray and so I did, mostly out of desperation. But as time wore on and things were not happening the way I envisioned I became discouraged with prayer. *Why am I praying? It's not making any difference. People say prayer changes things. Really? It's not happening in my world. I might as well be talking to the sky. It feels like that's where my prayers are going.* For a while, I did give up. That didn't last long as I reasoned I needed the communication even though I felt I wasn't getting anything from the other side. Maybe something would break through eventually.

Immediately after Scott's death my struggle with prayer intensified. I started reading everything I could about prayer, searching for what had gone wrong with my prayers. I'm not sure what exactly I was looking for, reasons why, maybe just comfort that others didn't have answers as well, perhaps, looking for justification that I didn't deserve His answer in the way I was looking for. Whatever it was, God used my search to turn my thinking completely around to *His* way of thinking about prayer. Through the next several months, He revealed Himself in amazing ways. I began to look at prayer in a whole different light. My relationship with Him was totally revolutionized.

However, I still had questions regarding prayer. I think most people who have a sudden traumatic event happen to them naturally ask that big "Why" question. I did, initially, but God made it very plain that I probably will never get a satisfactory answer to that this side of glory. I turned my attention to learning more about prayer. Through reading the scriptures and books others have written regarding their experiences, God began to change my attitude about prayer in so many ways.

First and foremost, He made it very clear that prayer was a command; we are to do it regardless of circumstances or feelings. We are to pray and trust Him for the answer, whatever that answer might be. He works behind the scenes to bring about His purpose in all He puts us through. I have a vivid reminder of this.

One of the few art endeavors I undertook is a very simple needlepoint. I was very diligent in my work, trying to make every stitch just right. Concentrating on the front of that needlepoint, I was pleased with my progress. When I finished with the front, I had to look at the back to put a backing on it. I am so glad that side isn't hanging on my wall. It's not a pretty picture. There are threads going every which way, knots here and there, and mixed up colors that don't make sense.

When I was going through all those struggles, I was looking at the back side of God's design. I only saw the tangled threads and felt the knots in my way. I couldn't see how any of this made sense. The colors were all messed up and everything was going wrong. But God says in Isaiah 55:8,9 that my thoughts and ways and His thoughts and ways are different. His are obviously higher than mine. I couldn't see how any of these things He was putting in my way were making any sense. It took me a long time to even begin to see the picture from the other side. When I left my prayers and faith to Him alone, I did, indeed, find that His will is wiser than my own. He has the total picture in His thoughts and is weaving it through my life. I had to trust that He had a beautiful plan in His mind, even though I got stuck in the tangles. I am beginning to catch a glimpse of that picture He is still creating. I can sit back and enjoy my piece of art, now that it is completed. It is especially meaningful as the words on the needlepoint say, "Life is fragile, handle with prayer."

Many times God has given me problems in my life, small to begin with, to allow me to seek a solution. I eventually realized He had the answer and I needed to trust Him.

My computer and I are on a need-to-know basis only, since I'm not a techie. When something doesn't go the way I want or think it should when I am on the computer I get distressed. My conversation with my computer is less than edifying and I quickly seek the nearest resource to help.

I encountered this situation a lot when designing a new weight-training notebook for my class. Fortunately, a person close by showed me what I was doing wrong and walked me through the correction. The next time I came to that problem I was not nearly as upset because I now had the answer.

I believe all those smaller troubles in my life allowed me to see that God not only had the answer, *He was the answer.* I needed to trust Him fully, no matter what I saw happening. I still struggle with those little problems that crop up. He puts those faith tests there so I may have the confidence He's still at work, transforming me into the person He wants me to become. If that's the "method rare" to keep me soaring with Him, then I am on my way to "counting it all joy."

Chapter 23

AND NOW

Do not call to mind the former things,
or ponder things of the past.
Behold, I will do something new,
now it will spring forth;
will you not be aware of it?
Isaiah 43:18,19a (NASB)

Time heals all wounds. Whoever said that must not have lost a child, or for that matter, a close loved one. There is always a hole in your heart that will not heal. However, I do feel that God has wept over every suture He used to repair my broken heart. As a loving Father, He knew this loss would cause me pain but He also knew it would draw me closer to Him. Yes, He's put my heart back together so that I may cherish and love the memories of Scott, but time will never completely heal the emptiness that the wound has caused.

But life does go on. I count myself fortunate that God has walked so close to me during the years since Scott's death. The lessons I've learned could not have been learned any other way. Do I wish they could have? Most certainly. But God most assuredly knows best and I will leave the results with Him.

The previous chapters have taken you through many things God has revealed to me about Him. But I would like to share some more attitudes God gave me afterward, toward others, as well as myself. One change is in the way I approach my students.

Like so many people, I unfortunately had a tendency to judge people by their outward appearance. As much as I would like to say I treated everyone alike, I put students in categories. If they dressed extraordinarily, had tattoos, or sported outlandish-colored hair, I tended to either write them off as nonconformist or not pay attention to them. They were different, so I didn't know what to do with them. I thought maybe they would be confrontational and I couldn't handle that. I would tend to be less engaging with them as I would with the other students.

Scott certainly fell into this category of being "out of the norm." He was clearly a boy but dressing and appearing as a girl. However, God started to change my outlook. Underneath the outer appearance there was still the son I loved. His heart was still the same. Not too long after his death, I had a wonderful dream that brought this to my attention. I could make out Scott's face, so I knew it was he, but he was neither male nor female and he was dressed with clothing more of light than cloth. That image stayed in my mind for a long time. I needed to remember that in God's eyes we are neither male nor female, black nor white, conformist nor nonconformist. We are all the same underneath those exterior coverings. Beneath all of that is a heart that God yearns to be in fellowship with. Jesus died for everyone, not just the ones who look like me. Because of that dream, I became very convicted about the judgment I was imposing on those around me.

Since then, I have had the privilege of engaging in some quite profound conversations with these students who look different than I. Getting to know them has been fun and eye-opening. It has allowed me to open myself up and be more real with them. Some of these folks have turned out to be amazing people. Some I have been able to counsel and witness to.

Deylon was a student with an attitude. I shied away from him. It appeared he didn't want to be in the class but would suffer through it. He did his workout but wasn't very sociable. I finally got my act together and approached him. We got into a conversation, starting out with what he needed to do for the class, because he had some missing work. But the conversation turned into learning he was dealing with family members on drugs and in rehab and didn't have a stable living situation. As we talked he began to soften up. I talked with him about spiritual things and encouraged him to stay in school. I have not seen him since, but I pray God used that short interlude to affect his life in a positive way.

My constant prayer is that God will allow me the opportunity to speak with them and for me to be a voice for Him. When these opportunities happen, I take advantage of them, knowing God has put us together for a purpose. Nothing is a coincidence in God's world.

Realizing God does nothing by accident is another concept that God has impressed upon me. I'm sure most people who have experienced a sudden loss will agree that we awaken to the fact that time is never guaranteed. I left for a conference that weekend fully expecting to see my son when I got home. My mind was not fully on the conference since I was thinking about Scott and how much I loved him. Some of those last conversations were playing back in my mind. *Should I have said something different? Did he know how much I really loved him?* Those and so many other questions were never answered. He was forever gone before I had the opportunity to express my love one more time. I have since learned to listen to that still, small voice that God uses to prompt me to do something. I need to do it *then*, not wait for another time. There have been too many times when there never was another moment. I have bruises on my backside from the times I've kicked myself for not heeding those nudges and knowing I just let another chance go by. This applies to witnessing, helping someone in need, or talking with someone in a grocery store or a waiting room. Continuing to recognize God is in the details of my life and nothing is an accident has helped me get in tune with where He is working and how He can use me in any situation.

Control. That word has been used many times in this book. I guess it's just our nature to want to take charge. There are things that are within our realm of control and things that are not. We can control what we do with our time. The food we eat is a matter of choice. What we think is maybe not as easy to manage but still controllable. Clearly these fall into the category of regulated circumstances. The problems occur with situations that aren't so easy to deal with, "unforeseeable circumstances" that force us to change our plans. The weather is certainly something we can't control, illustrated by the famous saying, "Everybody complains about the weather but nobody does anything about it." Yes, we can complain about these uncontrollable things or we can accept them and move on. We can change our attitude because we know we can't do a thing about the circumstances. We can't control other people just like we can't control the weather. But many people think they do have the capability to control others. It took me a long time before I realized I was one of those people.

In many instances I maintained that if I presented all the right information to somebody they surely would come around to my point of view or do what I wanted or expected them to do. Of course, I gave them only the information I wanted them to have to lead them to the expected outcome. People will make up their own minds and do their own thing with what is given. I can get upset about that or I can change my attitude and get on with my own life. I wanted my outcome so much in so many people's lives, particularly Scott's, that I missed a major lesson God was teaching me.

One of the jobs of the Holy Spirit is to convict people of sin, according to John 16. I was not relying on Him to do His job. I was relying on myself and getting very uptight about what I was saying and doing. I felt it was totally up to me to say all the right things and cover all the bases, putting myself under an unnecessary burden. I finally had to give up control and let God work in Scott's life, and, for that matter, everybody else's. Jim, my counselor, kept telling me that Scott definitely had his own free will and would exercise it, no matter what information was given him. Since then, I have learned to trust His leading not only in my own life but in the lives of others. My responsibility is to be true to what He has led me to say and let it go. He's a big God and doesn't need my help to do His job. It has freed me of guilt.

William Allen White said, "I am not afraid of tomorrow, for I have seen yesterday and I love today." For many years I lived in the fear of "what if." Early in my Christian life I was fearful that God would send me to a place where I didn't want to go. *What if God sent me to a desolate place? What would I do? Would I be ready? Would I be able to handle it?* The doubts were many. The years and "what ifs" went on. My mind would soar down the road, ahead of the present circumstances, and project what might happen. *What if I didn't choose the right husband? Would I be happy? What if I didn't get the job I wanted? What kind of job would I get? What if I got injured and couldn't lift weights or exercise anymore?* That's where my mind would finally stop since I couldn't fathom all the possibilities of these scenarios. Of course, my biggest fear was about Scott and his death. Those last months before he died I couldn't help going continually down the path of thinking *What if he actually took his life?* I didn't want to think about it but couldn't stop. The fear, the constant nagging of that thought, was always in my head—consciously or unconsciously. Then it happened. My worst fear was realized. I didn't know how to handle the fact that it had actually taken place. But I had to come to terms with the real circumstances. However, in spite of all this, I woke up the next morning; I was still alive. Yes, things were vastly different in my world but I found I could still put one foot in front of the other. I got through that day, and then another, taking each day with its problems to be worked through. Now God has taken away my fear of being unprepared.

As time went on, I have found William White's words to be very applicable. I don't fear tomorrow because I have been through the worst yesterday of my life. I can look back and see how God provided everything I needed to get me through each moment of those days I thought I couldn't endure. During my dark days, a song that speaks of how God holds all our tomorrows kept running through my mind. *I don't know about tomorrows, but I know for sure who holds my hand going through all those tomorrows.* He taught me that fretting about what might happen is worthless and needless expended energy. God has His plans and He has provisions for me in whatever He has in store for me in those plans. I can love today, knowing He is there. I can be free to enjoy whatever He has for me at this moment. It's a major step forward in my journey to "counting it all joy!"

Chapter 24

Moving On

O Lord, Thou art my God;
I will exalt Thee,
I will give thanks to Thy name;
for Thou has worked wonders,
plans formed long ago,
with perfect faithfulness.
Proverbs 25:1

Many lessons learned, more to come. I know the facts of those promises He gave are for *me to use*, not just nice words on a page to memorize. They have real meaning and application. I need to take God, literally, at His word. That has made the biggest impact on me through this whole journey. I read my Bible with new eyes and intensity. My walk with Him is profoundly personal, knowing everything He has done in my life has meaning and purpose. I can look to the future with a freedom not experienced before because I know it's in His hands, not mine.

Do I still make mistakes? Absolutely. I haven't walked on water yet, so I know I'm not perfect. Do I still have doubts? Certainly. I still wrestle from time to time with what He's doing and how He's dealing with a situation. I don't have all the answers and never will. I'm still growing in my faith and He is continually giving me new tests just to let me know that I haven't learned it all. Guilt frequently rears its ugly head. It wants to take over my thoughts and tell me that I had failed Scott and somehow caused his death. I have a natural reaction to fear and get anxious in certain conditions.

Driving on snowy, icy roads sometimes gets me tense. I like to test myself on the ski slopes, going down a little steeper hill than I'm used to just to face my fears. I will admit a whispered prayer is breathed just before I head down, though. In all these situations, God brings me back to Him, reassuring me. That's when I know I am living in His strength, not mine.

There's a great line in the movie *Meatballs*. Bill Murray's character is giving his underdog squad of misfits a pep rally to inspire them to play a very sophisticated team in football. He tells them, "It just doesn't matter" if they win or lose and they get behind him. That has often been my mantra. I look at the details in my life. They could be minor or major health problems, money problems, or relationships not going right. I stop and think, in the perspective of all that has happened and all the major calamities occurring around me, these things don't really matter. God knows about all these things and has them in His hand. God has called me to a purpose to glorify him and

He can take care of the smallest of details as well as the exploding events taking place in my life and the world. He has worked everything out already. I need to remember that. Remembering that line reminds me I just need to be faithful in doing what He has called me to do at any given time.

I will always miss my son. There is not a day goes by that I don't think about him in some way. The bitter memories are starting to fade, while the pleasant memories are becoming sweeter. My heart will always yearn for his presence. I found a poem he wrote while in high school. I keep it on my desk not only to remind me of him but to remember the last line.

I LIVE

I chase rainbows in the springtime
And colored leaves in the fall.
I catch snowflakes in December
When the weather gets so cold
And in the summer I watch clouds
As I sit atop a hill beneath a tree
Wondering what life has to bring
As the seasons cycle year to year.

I attend school everyday
At a prompt time of nine
I see each teacher for each class
As they speak their words to me
And when I leave at two o'clock
I sometimes think about the day
Other times what I have left,

The homework I haven't done.

Friday night rolls round each week
And I clap my hands with glee
When I hang with friends
Who like me just for me
We play games and have good times
As the night drains away
Then I wake up the next day
And love that it is Saturday.

My eyes find strains of light
Refracting in the sand, and on a beach
I find the sun setting a glass in my hand
I find the greatest things in life
All too often are not what costs the most
But those things that really are truly free.

Returning from a walk I still anticipate seeing his bike in
the driveway when I turn the corner on our street. I loved seeing him on his bicycle seat with his honey-colored hair streaming from beneath his cat hat. Even the aroma of his perspira-
tion after riding home from work would be pleasant to me. I
admired that he could make that arduous trip of over five miles
uphill seem like nothing. When I hear the song "Delilah" on
the car radio, I see him humming and singing along as he sat
beside me in the car. He would take whatever was handy to
use as a microphone, a pencil or even a shoe. Sometimes in the
kitchen I can feel his arms hugging me tightly around my waist
while I'm at the sink. He would come from behind and squeeze

as tightly as he could, causing me to lose my breath. And of course, I miss him saying my most favorite word in the whole, wide world, "Mom."

Scott's short journey on earth is complete. God welcomed him home where he is free from any pain and in the arms of Jesus. My journey continues, my story yet to be finished. As with Scott, my journey will not end until I take that final step into glory, meeting my Savior, and my son, face-to-face. So, see ya then, Bug.

Chapter 25

FOLLOW-UP

And we know that God causes
all things to work together
for good to those who love God,
to those who are called
according to His purpose.
Romans 8:28

Transgender. Gender dysphoria. Transsexual. These terms being bantered about in our society have become all too common. Many changes have taken place since Scott's death in 2009. Unfortunately, the statement that Devon Williams and Jeff Johnson's predicted concerning this, "*the next big wave in terms of adolescent development*" have come true. Today's worldview has embraced this type of activity; the government has endorsed it through insurance coverage, the media certainly has paid much attention, and even the schools have validated it in offering classes and accommodating students who are transitioning. Parents are urged to recognize early symptoms and encouraged to start their children on hormones. Yes, the world has gone overboard, it seems, in making sure the transgendered person is accepted into today's society.

Previously, it was considered a disorder. That is no longer the case. Rather than a disorder, it is now termed gender dysphoria. Not content with merely being tolerated by society the transgendered now want affirmation with transgender equality.

The medical and psychiatric professions are under pressure to promote the transgender agenda, even against research and their personal moral obligations.

Johns Hopkins University was one of the first medical institutions to provide transitional surgeries in 1965. However, after doing long-term follow-up studies with transgendered patients they found the surgeries did not produce the quality of life expected after ten years or more. Suicide rates were many times higher than the general population. As a result, they discontinued the procedure in 1979. Now under pressure from the transgender community, they have reinstated the practice. Psychiatrists can no longer offer counseling against becoming transgender to children who may be taking that path, even with parental consent. Even though the research shows that early hormone therapy is harmful to growth and reproductive capability, it is still advocated. Studies also show that young children who exhibit transgender behavior will most often be restored to natural gender feelings with no intervention, particularly because the brain does not fully develop until age twenty-four. Denise Shick, with Help 4 Families (with whom I was in contact early on) reports she is dealing with more parents of younger children. The current is definitely getting stronger and picking up speed for those who choose to swim against it. As bleak as the picture may seem there is still hope! We cannot give up because *"greater is He that is in you than he who is in the world."* (1 John 4:4b) and *"with God all things are possible."* (Matthew 19:26)

If you find yourself in the midst of this struggle, consider your hope. The word hope, as it is used in scripture, means *confidence* that God will see you through. What can we have confidence in?

1. The character of God. Who and what God is. To name just a few, He is omnipresent, omnipotent, omniscient, truth, and love. Always remember how much He loves you and your loved one. As long as you are both alive He has a plan and purpose for you. Take a hard look at *all* God is and *know* He can handle all your problems.

2. Prayer. It is your lifeline. "Call unto Me and *I will answer you* . . ." (Jeremiah 33:3) Even though it feels like God is not listening, we have confidence that He is listening and will answer. Don't be afraid to cry out, to be angry and frustrated with God. He knows how you're feeling and He can take all you throw at Him. Go back through the chapter on prayer and review the scriptures.

3. His word. As you call out to God, don't forget the other half of the conversation. Look at His promises He's given. God cannot lie. If He's said it He means it and will carry it out. God uses His word to teach, comfort, and exhort us. Immerse yourself with scripture; study it, memorize it, meditate on it, but most of all *believe* it. The scriptures I've mentioned throughout the previous chapters are the ones that I "have hid in my heart." They have given me great confidence through the years.

4. Support. Know that you are not alone. Others will come alongside you as you walk through this valley. Just as Aaron and Hur supported Moses' arms in the battle, so there are those who will uphold you. Your pastor, people in your church, Bible study groups, prayer partners, are all people God has put into your life to help you. I also recommend Denise's website, www.help4families.com. It is a wonderful resource for comfort and counsel. It also includes numerous testimonies of those who have come out of transgenderism.

God is in the business of redemption. He can redeem your loved one and He can redeem you, to bring you into a deeper relationship with Himself. This is not something *you* are going to fix for the person involved. God is in control -give Him the reins and let Him handle it.

> *I waited intently for the Lord;*
> *And He inclined to me, and heard my cry.*
> *He brought me up out of the pit of destruction,*
> *out of the miry clay;*
> *And He set my feet upon a rock*
> *making my footsteps firm.*
> *And He put a new song in my mouth,*
> *a song of praise to our God;*
> *Many will see and fear,*
> *And will trust in the Lord.*
> *Psalm 40:1-3 (NASB)*

ORDER INFORMATION

REDEMPTION
PRESS

To order additional copies of this book, please visit
www.redemption-press.com.
Also available on Amazon.com and BarnesandNoble.com
Or by calling toll free 1-844-2REDEEM.